ONTARIO BIGFOOT

Ghosts in the Darkness — Series

By Timothy D

True Encounters, Field Notes, and Wilderness Investigations Across Canada's Wild North

Ontario Bigfoot is part of the *Ghosts in the Darkness* series: A collection of real-world investigations into unexplained wilderness phenomena, written by a field researcher who has spent over 15 years exploring Canada's most remote forests, lakes, and northern terrain.

Timothy D
Northern Ontario Wilderness Researcher & Author

Copyright Page

ONTARIO BIGFOOT
Ghosts in the Darkness — Series

© *2025 by **Timothy D***
All rights reserved.

No part of this publication may be reproduced, distributed, or transmitted in any form or by any means, including photocopying, recording, or other electronic or mechanical methods, without the prior written permission of the author, except in the case of brief quotations embodied in critical reviews and certain other noncommercial uses permitted by copyright law.

Ghosts in the Darkness Series

This is a work of non-fiction. Witness statements, field notes, and investigative descriptions are based on the author's real experiences, interviews, and collected case files. Some identifying details have been altered to respect privacy. All interpretations and conclusions belong solely to the author.

Cover design: *Ghosts in the Darkness Creative*
Interior layout: *Timothy D*
Series branding: *Ghosts in the Darkness*

First Edition.

ISBN: 978-1-0696715-8-5

INTRODUCTION
What the Wilderness Has Taught Me

By Timothy D

There's a moment every time I step into the bush—usually somewhere between the last pickup truck on the highway and the first silence of the deep woods—when something shifts. It's subtle, but unmistakable. The air cools. The wind settles. The noise of the human world fades until it feels like it never existed at all.

And then the forest starts paying attention.

Some people call it solitude. Some call it peace. But over the years I've come to understand it as something else—awareness. Not mine—*theirs*. The sense that the land is watching, listening, deciding what to reveal and what to hide.

When I first began exploring Ontario's backcountry, I wasn't looking for anything extraordinary. I was looking for space, quiet, the kind of stillness that only exists north of the pavement. But the more time I spent out there, the more I realized that the forest was holding onto secrets—old ones, deep ones, whispered ones.

And eventually, those secrets began revealing themselves.

Not all at once.
Not dramatically.
But in quiet, steady patterns.

A knock on a tree where no person should be.
A howl that didn't match any known animal.
Footprints pressed deep into the moss—too large, too heavy, too

precise.
Moments of stillness that felt like being watched.
Moments of sound that made me question everything I thought I knew.

This book is about those patterns, and what they've taught me.

What I've Learned in the Wilderness

Fifteen years in Ontario's north will change a person. It changed me—not because of the strange encounters, but because of how those encounters forced me to pay attention.

Here's what I've learned, in the simplest and truest way I can say it:

1. The forest is not empty.

Not in Algonquin.
Not in Temagami.
Not in Sudbury, North Bay, Kenora, or the James Bay frontier.
Something moves out there—something large, quiet, deliberate, and intelligent.

2. Bigfoot sightings in Ontario are not rare.

They are consistent.
Steady.
Predictable by region.
And reported by people who know the land better than their own living rooms.

3. Whatever this creature is, it knows how to avoid us.

It moves like a shadow between lakes and ridges.
It uses waterways like highways.
It avoids open areas but will approach camps if it wants to.
It observes without revealing itself—unless it chooses to.

4. The sounds are what stay with you.

The deep, resonant howls in Algonquin.
The "mumbling" phenomenon in Temagami.
The sudden knocks echoing through the Sudbury backcountry.
The screams in Rabbit Lake that you feel in your chest.

Sound travels differently up here. It carries farther, deeper, and with more weight.
And although I've heard wolves, moose, foxes, bears, owls, and everything else this land can produce, some sounds still sit outside the range of explanation.

5. Tracks don't lie.

People do.
Stories do.
Memories do.
But the ground does not.
And the number of large, consistent, anatomically correct trackways I've seen across Ontario is too high to dismiss.

6. The farther north you go, the more the land changes—and so does the activity.

In places like James Bay, Longlac, Fort Hope, and the muskeg corridors, the sightings become bolder.
The prints become larger.
And the distances between encounters shrink.

7. The key to understanding Bigfoot isn't belief—

it's pattern recognition.**

Once you see the patterns, you cannot unsee them.

Why This Book Matters

This book isn't a collection of campfire tales or urban legends.
It's a record of what I've encountered, what others have shown me, and what the land itself seems determined to reveal if you spend enough nights listening to it breathe.

It is a field report—written by someone who has walked the trails, heard the sounds, followed the prints, and spent years trying to make sense of the shadows between the trees.

I'm not interested in convincing anyone.
I'm interested in documenting the truth of what exists out there, regardless of who accepts it.

Every chapter in this book is rooted in real reports, real sightings, real evidence, and the real wilderness of Ontario.
Some chapters will take you deep into familiar forests.
Others will drag you into regions almost no one ever visits.

By the time you finish this book, you may not believe everything I've seen.
But you may start to understand why I keep returning to these places—why the mystery pulls harder each year, and why the land feels alive in a way most people never experience.

Where Our Journey Begins

It starts where it should—
in the center of one of Canada's most ancient landscapes:

Algonquin Provincial Park.

A place where voices echo through the pines long after midnight.
A place where howls drift across lakes in tones too deep and too controlled to be wolves.
A place where, in 2009, a strange figure stepped out of the brush near the North Gate and was caught on video.
A place layered with decades of unusual sounds, sightings, and unexplained encounters.

Algonquin is not just a wilderness.
It is a threshold.
A place where the known world blurs into the unknown.

And that is where our story begins.

Table Of Contents

1. Introduction — What I've Learned in the Wilderness

Regional Chapters

2. Algonquin Provincial Park
3. Temagami: The Dark Heart of the North
4. Sudbury: The Northern Crossroads
5. North Bay & Nipissing District
6. Cochrane District
7. Kenora & The Far Northwest
8. Thunder Bay Region
9. Sault Ste. Marie & The Algoma Triangle
10. Durham County & the Southern Fringe
11. Eastern Ontario
12. Parry Sound District
13. Southwest Counties
14. Simcoe County
15. Muskoka
16. Kawartha Lakes

17. Haliburton Highlands

18. Hastings County

19. Lennox & Addington

20. Peterborough County

21. Frontenac County

22. Ottawa Valley

23. The St. Lawrence & Thousand Islands Wilderness

24. The Niagara Escarpment

25. Manitoulin Island

26. Georgian Bay & The Killarney Coastline

27. The French River & Nipissing Corridor

28. The Mattawa Valley & Deep East

29. Ontario's Bigfoot Corridors: A Province-Wide Movement Pattern

30. Field Technology: How We Investiagate The Impossible

31. Hoaxes, Misidentifications & The Fringe Cases

Appendix A — Ontario Bigfoot Sightings Database (Expanded)

Appendix B — Indigenous Lore & Historical Accounts

Acknowledgements

1 — ALGONQUIN: VOICES IN THE PINES

There is a sound in Algonquin that everyone who spends enough time there eventually hears—a long, hollow note carried across the trees, resonant enough to feel in your chest but distant enough that you're never quite certain where it came from. It's part wind, part echo, part instinctive warning system telling you the forest is older and stranger than you thought.

It's the kind of sound that makes you stop mid-step, tilt your head, and whisper, *What the hell was that?*

That's the beginning of this story.

Not a sighting.
Not a footprint.
A sound.

Because in Algonquin Provincial Park, the mystery begins with what you hear long before you ever see anything.

The park is enormous—7,600 square kilometres of deep wilderness, lakes, ridges, and bush so thick you could step off a trail and vanish from the world. It's old too—much older than most people realize. The bedrock here is ancient shield stone, and the forests that grow on top of it have been rising, falling, burning, and regenerating for millennia.

Algonquin is a place where the land remembers things.

And where, for as long as anyone has dared to talk about it, something has been making noises that don't belong to any known animal.

I didn't start my research career here. But like most people who've spent years chasing strange reports across Ontario, I eventually found myself standing at one of the park's many trailheads, listening to a stillness that felt a little too heavy—not dangerous, just aware.

What I didn't know then was that Algonquin would set the tone for everything that followed.

The North Gate Sighting — 2009

The moment everything shifted

The case that first pushed Algonquin into the modern Bigfoot conversation happened in 2009 near the park's North Gate. A man driving down the access road spotted a large, dark figure moving through the underbrush. He did something most people don't—he grabbed a camera and filmed it.

The video isn't perfect.
They never are.

But it's clear enough to show:

- a tall, upright figure
- moving on two legs
- with a broad stride
- disappearing into thick brush

To this day, the footage sits in that gray zone between undeniable and uncertain—the space where most Bigfoot evidence lives. But the important part is this:

The man wasn't looking for Bigfoot.
He wasn't a believer.
He wasn't chasing shadows.
He filmed what he saw because it was *there*.

That's the pattern with Algonquin reports.
They come from fishermen, hikers, hunters, canoeists—not from people seeking encounters.

The forest decides who sees what, and when.

And in 2009, it decided to show itself.

July 2020 — The Madawaska Valley Howls

A call that made researchers stop everything

In July 2020, audio experts analysis circulated after chilling howls were recorded in the Madawaska Valley—southeast of Algonquin but well within the ecosystem's reach.

The sound was deep, projecting miles across water.

It wasn't a wolf.
Not even close.

Experienced outdoorsmen listened and compared it to known species. Nothing matched. It had the long, rising cadence of a primate call—not the frantic pitch of a predator, but the measured projection of something built to communicate over distance.

When I heard the recording for the first time, it hit me in the same way all real evidence does: not as a mystery, but as familiarity. A kind of deep recognition. The sound pattern was consistent with other calls recorded in remote areas of Ontario.

Algonquin doesn't shout at you.
It calls.
And those calls are becoming harder to ignore.

July 2009 — The Thud in the Pines

When a single sound can change the mood of the forest

Two hikers in July 2009 reported hearing an unusual *thud*—a sudden, heavy impact — followed by a short, low whoop that didn't resemble any known animal. They said it was like "a hand hitting a hollow log" followed by the kind of soft vocalization you'd expect from a primate, not a predator.

But the detail that matters most is what came after:

They felt watched.

There's a quality to that sensation that doesn't translate well on paper. It's not paranoia. It's not fear. It's an instinct you feel in your spine before your brain catches up. Hunters know it. Experienced trappers know it. Anyone who's spent enough time alone in deep bush knows it.

It's the moment your senses expand—not outwards, but inwards. Your body becomes the antenna.

Algonquin produces this feeling more than almost any place I've ever been.

The whoop mattered.
The thud mattered.
But the silence that followed?
That was the part that stuck with them.

1995 — The Aylen Lake Howl

The one old-timers still talk about

Aylen Lake sits on the eastern edge of the park—a quiet corridor where thick pines press against the shoreline and the darkness arrives earlier than it should.

In 1995, campers reported hearing a deep, sustained howl echo across the lake. Not the high-pitched scream of a fox or the moaning wail of a moose, but something chest-deep, almost whale-like in its resonance. A sound too heavy and too controlled to be anything common.

People still talk about this howl today.

Not because of what it sounded like—but because of how it *felt*.

Sound is physics, but the human body doesn't experience it that way.
Some sounds feel like warnings.
Some feel like invitations.
Some feel like announcements.

This howl felt like a boundary marker.

A territorial claim.

And it was powerful enough that two separate groups of campers filed independent reports.

Algonquin is vast enough that something could vocalize loudly and never be seen.
But the sound becomes the evidence.
The forest carries it farther than any footprint.

The Thing About Algonquin Is This

If I had to sum up the park's Bigfoot activity in one sentence, it would be this:

Algonquin whispers before it reveals.

Most regions in Ontario give you tracks first.
Some give you movement.
Some give you glimpses.

Algonquin gives you sound.
And with sound comes pattern.

The same types of calls emerge in these woods year after year, decade after decade:

- long howls
- deep resonant calls
- heavy thuds
- soft whoops
- wood knocks

- strange "conversation-like" sequences
- and the unmistakable sensation of being observed

These patterns match worldwide Bigfoot hotspots.

They also align with something more subtle — geography.

Because Algonquin isn't isolated.
It's connected by waterways, valleys, and ridgelines to:

- Madawaska
- Barry's Bay
- Whitney
- South River
- Sundridge
- Kearney
- North Bay
- Temagami

Creatures using these corridors could move silently through enormous territory.

And they seem to.

Why Algonquin's Evidence Is Harder to Find

Algonquin's soil is poor for footprints.
Its trails are rocky.
Its logging roads drain well.
Its moss is too shallow for clear impressions.
And its backcountry is too vast for most people to explore far beyond the first portage.

Tracks vanish quickly here.
Sound lingers.

That's why the park is known more for vocalizations than visuals.

But make no mistake — visuals do occur.
And when they do, they matter.

The 2009 video matters.
The 1995 howl matters.
The 2009 whoop matters.
The 2020 recordings matter.

Strange patterns don't occur in a vacuum.

They occur in ecosystems where the land becomes the perfect hiding place.

Algonquin is exactly that.

A Forest That Watches Back

My first time hearing something I couldn't explain in Algonquin wasn't dramatic.
It wasn't a roar or a scream.
It wasn't something charging through the brush.

It was a knock.

One single, sharp knock from somewhere up a ridge. Not a falling branch, not a hunter's signal, not the sharp crack of ice shifting. Just one deliberate strike.

Then silence.

The kind of silence that feels like a held breath.

I remember thinking:

If that was a person, why just once?
If that was an animal, why so clean and hollow?
And if it wasn't either... what am I listening to?

That was the moment I knew this wasn't just a hobby or curiosity.
It was a study.
A lifetime study.

Something lives in these woods.
Something strong.
Something intelligent.
Something cautious.
Something already well-adapted to avoiding humans.

And Algonquin is one of its sanctuaries.

Why We Start Here

We begin this book in Algonquin because this park is the doorway into the phenomenon. The place where:

- the sounds are clearest

- the sightings are credible

- the wilderness is deep

- and the patterns are undeniable

Algonquin doesn't give you a monster.
It doesn't give you a myth.
It gives you behaviour.

And behaviour is evidence.

Sightings can be debated.
Videos can be argued.
Stories can be embellished.

But behaviour—especially repeat behaviour—tells you something is real.

In Algonquin, the behaviour has been repeating for decades.

This is where the mystery becomes something more than campfire talk.
This is where the forest begins to speak.

And this is where our journey starts—not with answers, but with the voices that call across the pines after midnight.

The kind of voices that make you stop, hold your breath, and ask yourself the question every investigator eventually faces:

What else is out there?

CHAPTER 2 — TEMAGAMI: THE DARK HEART OF THE NORTH

Temagami changes you.

You don't realize it at first. The transformation isn't obvious. It starts quietly—on the drive north, somewhere past Marten River, when the world outside the windshield shifts from farmland and highway shoulders to towering red pines and blackwater lakes. Then the land begins to rise, folding into the kind of hills that feel ancient, almost sentient. The air cools. The sky darkens. The forest tightens around the road until it feels like you're being swallowed.

Temagami is not just another wilderness.
It's a presence.

There are places where the land feels empty, and places where it feels alive. Temagami is neither. Temagami feels *inhabited*. There's a weight to it—an old, quiet awareness that's hard to describe until you've spent enough time out there alone.

In this chapter, we're not starting with a single sighting or encounter.
We're starting with a place.
A place that has shaped every year of my field experience.
A place where the sightings cluster thick and heavy.
A place that has given Ontario some of its most important Bigfoot evidence.

Temagami is the pulse of northern mystery—steady, strong, and impossible to ignore.

An Ancient Land That Remembers

Before we get to the reports, you have to understand the land itself.

Temagami is home to some of the last remaining old-growth red and white pine forests in North America. Massive trees that predate European contact. Lakes so deep and clear they carry sound differently. Ridges of granite shaped by ice and wind and time. Miles of canoe routes winding into valleys and inland seas.

This is the kind of country where something large could live undetected—not for years, but for generations.

The terrain lends itself to secrecy:

- thick forest cover

- endless water corridors

- high ridgelines with long sightlines

- deep ravines for movement

- vast distances between human settlements

People don't stumble across Temagami by accident.
They seek it out, or they're born into it.

And for decades, those who've walked this land have reported seeing something that should not exist.

Let's start with one of the most important cases in all of Ontario.

2017–Present — The West Temagami Hunting Family Encounters

The backbone of modern Temagami sightings

Exploring Temagami's Bigfoot activity without mentioning the West Temagami hunting family would be like studying the Pacific Northwest without the Patterson–Gimlin film. This case is that significant.

Beginning in 2017, a multi-generational hunting family — who return to the same area every fall — started experiencing unusual activity around their remote camp.

The first year was subtle:

- heavy footsteps circling their camp at night
- branches snapping at shoulder height
- brief glimpses of dark shapes moving between trees
- a strange "mumbling" sound after midnight
- the unmistakable feeling of being watched

The second year escalated:

- rhythmic wood knocks from two directions
- tracks pressed deep into moss
- a dark figure crossing a cut line at dawn
- tree breaks found in a pattern

- heavy pacing outside their wall tent

The third year produced what they later called "the scream."

It was long, rising, chest-deep—nothing like a wolf or a man. It stopped every conversation, every movement, every thought. They described the silence afterward as "total"—a vacuum that made the hair on their arms lift.

By the fourth and fifth years, the encounters were so consistent they began expecting something every season.

This is not just a sighting.
It is a relationship between place and presence.

Year after year, something comes back to that valley.
And so do they.

Patterns like this create the foundation for understanding behaviour.
Whatever is in Temagami, it has territory—and it protects it.

2009 — The Remote Cabin Photograph (Class A)

A rare moment of visual clarity

In 2009, a couple staying at a remote cabin deep in the Temagami backcountry captured what remains one of Ontario's most intriguing Class A photographs.

The encounter was simple:

They were sitting outside near dusk.
The treeline was quiet.
The lake was still.

Then something walked through the clearing.

A tall, upright figure — dark, broad, and fast.
Not a bear.
Not a human.
Not anything they'd ever seen before.

They snapped multiple photographs before it slipped back into the forest.

Investigators later compared the size of the creature to trees in the image.
Estimated height: over 7 feet.
Estimated stride length: over 4 feet.

The creature appears mid-stride in one frame, stepping over a fallen branch with ease. The arm swing is long and natural — nothing like a suited hoax or a misidentified animal.

Some cases linger in the community for years.
This is one of them.

I've spoken to people who reviewed the originals.
No one credible has ever dismissed them outright.

Temagami's wilderness is rugged and remote enough that a human hoaxer would need to hike miles through unforgiving terrain just to pull off a brief moment — not worth the trouble for no payoff.

This photograph feels authentic because it fits the land.
And in Temagami, authenticity hides in the stillness.

The Old Yellowtop Encounters (1906–1970)

The legend that refuses to die

Temagami's Bigfoot history goes far beyond modern reports.

The earliest known Temagami encounter dates back to 1906, when miners in Cobalt reported seeing a creature described as:

- 8 feet tall

- dark hair

- and a distinctive yellow patch on its head

They called it "Old Yellowtop."

It wasn't a one-off.

- In 1923, settlers saw the same creature near cattle.

- In 1947, schoolchildren claimed to see it near the highway.

- In 1970, three miners—including Amos Latrielle and Larry Cormack—reported seeing an enormous creature with a yellow crest near the Cobalt Lode Mine.

This is the only Bigfoot in Ontario with an identifying physical feature repeatedly reported across decades.

Some researchers consider Yellowtop folklore.
I don't.

Folklore doesn't produce consistent descriptions over 64 years.
People do.

And people—different people from different eras—kept seeing the same creature in the same region with the same unique marking.

If Bigfoot exists in Ontario, Yellowtop may have been a distinct individual—one that lived a long life in the Temagami–Cobalt corridor.

It's not myth.
It's memory.

2014 — The Rabbit Lake Screams

Pure terror cutting across still water

Rabbit Lake sits northeast of Temagami, tucked into a narrow valley where sound travels in strange ways. In 2014, campers reported hearing an unsettling series of shrill screams just after midnight.

Not fox.
Not coyote.
Not owl.

These screams were:

- deep

- powerful

- long

- and controlled

The timing between them was precise—almost mechanical.

What made this case so eerie wasn't the scream itself, but the aftermath.

The forest went dead silent.

Anyone who's spent enough nights in the wilderness knows that total silence is unnatural. A forest always hums—with insects, birds, branches shifting in the wind.

When the forest goes quiet, something is watching.

And that night, something was.

2014 — The Wilson Lake Vocals (Case 185-14)

A call and answer across Temagami's old water routes

Just months after Rabbit Lake, anglers on Wilson Lake heard a long, rising howl that faded into a low moan. The sound drifted across the water like a warning—or a call.

What makes this case important is its similarity to vocalizations recorded in the Adirondacks, the Pacific Northwest, and Alaska.

Temagami doesn't produce random noise.
It produces *patterns*.

And Wilson Lake fits those patterns perfectly.

2011 — Lake Temagami Growls and Screams (Case 102-11)

A phone interview that still sends chills

In July 2011, a witness reported hearing growls and screaming sounds near Lake Temagami during a late-night outing. The witness said the sound was "massive," like a creature with a chest large enough to hold resonance beyond anything known in Ontario wildlife.

The growls were described as low, guttural, and intelligent—almost a warning response.

The screams that followed were sharp, rising, and projected.

In my experience, growls matter more than screams.
They indicate proximity.

Something was close that night—close enough that the witness felt the vibration.

When someone says "I felt it," you take the report seriously.

The forest doesn't vibrate without reason.

The Patterns of Temagami

When you arrange all Temagami-area encounters on a map, something very interesting happens:

The sightings line up along ancient travel corridors:

- Rabbit Lake
- Temagami Lake
- Wilson Lake
- Cassels Lake
- Marten River area
- Cobalt corridor
- The West Temagami valley

These aren't random dots—they're a network.

The creature (or creatures) of Temagami move in logical routes that follow:

- ridge lines
- water systems
- hidden valleys
- old trapline paths

This is the behaviour of a large, territorial, intelligent mammal.
Not a myth.
Not imagination.
Not folklore.

Pattern is evidence.

And Temagami is full of it.

What Temagami Has Taught Me

Of all the regions I've explored in Ontario, Temagami is the one that stays with me the most.
It's where the land feels oldest.
Where silence feels deepest.
Where shadows seem to linger a little too long.

Here's what this region has taught me:

1. These creatures have territories.

The West Temagami valley is one of them.

2. They revisit the same locations across years.

The behaviour around the hunting family proves it.

3. Temagami's sound signatures are consistent and unique.

The screams, howls, growls, and knocks match global patterns.

4. Old Yellowtop shows these creatures may live long lives—and be identifiable.

5. The land here supports a large, elusive primate far better than people realize.

6. Temagami is one of Ontario's Bigfoot epicentres.

Not because of legends, but because the evidence demands it.

Why Temagami Is the Heart of the Mystery

Algonquin whispers.
Sudbury watches.
Kenora shows itself.
James Bay intimidates.
Thunder Bay warns.

But Temagami?

Temagami *remembers*.

The land here holds onto things—footsteps, screams, shadows, stories. It's the one region where the encounters feel layered, almost historical. You're not just walking into a wilderness—you're walking into a place where something has been living for a very long time.

And you can feel it.

The deeper you go, the stronger it becomes.
The weight.
The presence.
The sense of something just out of view.

Temagami is the dark heart of the north because it pulses with mystery—steady, ancient, alive.

Whatever walks these forests walks with purpose.
Whatever watches from the treeline watches with intelligence.
And whatever left behind a century of sightings is still out there, moving between lakes and ridges like it owns the place.

Because maybe it does.

Temagami doesn't just hide Bigfoot.
Temagami is Bigfoot country.

And this is only the beginning.

CHAPTER 3 — SUDBURY: THE NORTHERN CROSSROADS

Sudbury doesn't look like a Bigfoot hotspot when you first drive into it. It looks like a mining town, a place of smokestacks, rail yards, and hard rock. But that's only the first impression—the surface version of Sudbury that most people see without ever stepping past the city limits.

Because once you drive ten minutes in any direction, Sudbury stops being a city.
And becomes something else entirely.

The north opens into Capreol and Cartier—long ridges, hidden lakes, endless spruce.
The west becomes Lively and Naughton—rock barrens, muskeg, silent forest.
The south dissolves into Burwash—abandoned lands reclaimed by wilderness.
And the east spills into Hanmer, Wahnapitae, and the old trapline country.

Sudbury sits in the middle of all of it.
A crossroads.
Not metaphorically—literally.

Creatures moving from Temagami can drop into Sudbury.
Creatures moving from North Bay can pass through Sudbury.
Creatures heading west toward Lake Superior can cut across Sudbury.

It is a junction point.
A nerve centre in Northern Ontario's wilderness.

And that alone would make it important.

But Sudbury has something else.

It has evidence.
More than most regions.
More than people expect.

This chapter covers every major Sudbury-area sighting—and what the land has taught me about why so many encounters happen here.

Why Sudbury Matters

Every region in Ontario has its own personality when it comes to encounters.

Algoquin whispers.
Temagami warns.
Kenora shows itself.
James Bay intimidates.

But Sudbury does something different.

Sudbury interacts.

It doesn't just produce sightings—it produces behaviours:

- rock throwing
- pacing
- trackways
- screams

- eyeshine

- road crossings

- territorial displays

- long-term cabin activity

These aren't isolated events.
They're region-wide patterns.

Sudbury is not just active — it's consistent.
And the land is a perfect amplifier for that activity.

The Canadian Shield rock forces animals to move along predictable routes.
The water systems act as corridors.
The ridges provide vantage points.
The marshes and alder thickets provide cover.

If something large and intelligent lived in Northern Ontario, it would use the Sudbury basin exactly the way we've documented.

And based on the number of sightings, it already does.

The Trout Lake Trackway — Winter 2013

The best Bigfoot trackway ever filmed in Ontario

Some cases define a region.
This one defines the entire Sudbury chapter.

In the winter of 2013, a family traveling near Trout Lake—just south of Sudbury—came across a long, untouched trackway pressed deep into fresh snow.

Not one track.
Not a handful.

Dozens.

The trackway was filmed from multiple angles.
Close-ups, wide shots, follow-along segments.
The family documented everything before snow or wind could change it.

What the footage shows is extraordinary:

- Perfect heel-to-toe impressions

- Clear toe splay visible in several prints

- No evidence of drag marks

- No human prints leading to or from

- A consistent, heavy weight distribution

- A stride far too long for a person

- Tracks aligned with natural terrain features

- Tracks continuing into forest too dense for a hoaxer to reach undetected

You can tell fake prints the moment you see them.
The gait is wrong.
The depth is wrong.
The anatomy is wrong.

But these were right.
Dead right.

Every print looked like it belonged to something with primate anatomy on a scale that should not exist.

What stays with me is not the footage itself—but how quiet the forest around it was.
The family describes the atmosphere as "heavy," almost "charged."

This trackway remains one of Ontario's most compelling pieces of physical evidence.

And it happened here, in Sudbury.

2013 — The Lively Balcony Sighting

A creature seen from a fourth floor apartment window

This is one of the strangest urban-edge sightings I've ever encountered.

A resident in Lively stepped onto their fourth-floor balcony one evening and noticed movement near the treeline. At first, they thought it was a bear. Then it stood upright.

Not briefly—fully.

The figure was tall, broad, and moving with smooth, confident strides between trees.

From the witness's vantage point, the creature was:

- larger than any human

- too upright and fluid to be a bear
- solid black
- silent
- aware of its surroundings

Urban sightings always interest me because they demonstrate a kind of boldness.
This creature approached the edge of a residential zone—quietly, deliberately, and without concern.

It didn't linger.
It didn't run.
It simply disappeared.

Sudbury creatures are not timid.
They move with intention—even near humans.

September 2015 — Capreol Watering Hole Sighting

When the forest paused

A group of hikers near Capreol approached a watering hole and saw a tall, dark figure standing at the opposite edge. The creature wasn't moving. It wasn't drinking. It was watching them.

They described:

- a height well over 7 feet
- a posture too human-like for any bear

- a broad, barrel-shaped torso
- long arms that hung low
- a stance of cautious curiosity

This was no fluke visual.
It was observation.

And the forest around the hikers went silent—the same kind of silence reported in Temagami and Algonquin during close-range encounters.

Silence is a signal.
Not to the creature—to you.

Something is there.
Something aware.

This sighting confirms a behavioural pattern across Sudbury: Observation from cover, from distance, followed by disappearance.

2015 — Killarney Screams & Running Figure

One of the clearest auditory encounters in Sudbury region

East of Sudbury, in the Killarney region, hikers heard a scream so deep and powerful it stopped them in their tracks. Seconds later a large figure ran through the trees.

The important part is *how* it moved:

- fast

- upright
- with long strides
- covering ground in seconds

The scream itself was described as:

- deep
- resonant
- projected
- unlike any known Ontario animal

The figure moved away immediately after the scream, suggesting:

- territorial display
- alarm call
- or sending a warning

Sudbury creatures often vocalize before or after movement—never during.
This is consistent with other primates.

Burwash — Rocks in the Dark (Case 194-13)

A territorial warning you do not ignore

The Burwash area is one of the strangest places in the Sudbury district—a reclaimed wilderness of old prison lands, thick bush, and haunting silence.

In 2012, hikers experienced one of Ontario's strongest territorial displays.

Large rocks—not small stones—began landing near them at dusk.

These rocks were:

- thrown
- with force
- from a concealed position

After they retreated, they found a freshly placed log blocking their exit trail—large enough that two grown men could not move it.

This was not opportunistic behaviour.
This was deliberate.

A creature:

- warned them
- chased them off
- blocked their escape path

This is textbook territorial primate behaviour.
Not random.
Not panicked.
Planned.

Sudbury's creatures are confident.
Territorial.
Strategic.

And Burwash is one of their strongholds.

2011 — Hanmer Dual-Encounter Campsite

One trip, two sightings, one long night

A group camping near Hanmer had two encounters on the same outing.

Encounter One: The Daylight Figure

They saw a tall, upright shape moving between trees late in the afternoon.

Encounter Two: The Night Pacing

That night, something circled their camp:

- heavy footsteps
- slow, steady pacing
- occasional pauses
- no vocalizations
- no attempts to approach
- no fear

The next morning, they found:

- deep impressions
- a path through the brush
- broken branches at 7–8 feet height

This is classic surveillance behaviour.
A creature monitoring humans without attempting contact.

Cartier 2014 — The Deep Vocalizations

A sound that traveled across ridgelines

Near Cartier, a witness heard long, resonant vocalizations echo across a ridge.

The call:

- began low
- rose slowly
- held tone
- carried for kilometres

Not wolf.
Not moose.
Not owl.

Cartier's acoustic geography allows sound to travel enormous distances.
The creature used that landscape perfectly.

These calls match Pacific Northwest recordings.

Which tells me this:

Whatever lives in Sudbury lives like its western counterparts— large lungs, large chest, controlled projection.

This was a creature communicating with another over distance. Not simply calling into the void.

Highway 6 Roadcrossing — Stratton Lake (146-13)

A creature running across the highway at full speed

One of Sudbury's most dramatic encounters occurred along Highway 6 near Stratton Lake in 2013.

A 25-year-old driver saw a massive black figure run across the road.

She described:

- a height of 10 feet
- an estimated weight of 300 pounds or more
- a speed unlike any human
- long, swinging arm movement

- two to three strides to cross the full road

- clearing the ditch in a single step

You do not get this wrong.
Not at night.
Not in headlights.
Not at that distance.

The witness was traumatized—but clear.

A creature that size does not exist in any field guide.

But it exists in Sudbury.

Spanish River Tracks (112-12)

Two canoeists find impossible footprints

Along the Spanish River, two canoeists found a set of large footprints at a portage.

The prints were:

- deep

- long

- anatomically correct

- evenly spaced

- preserved in mud

The Spanish is a natural travel corridor—an aquatic highway connecting vast pieces of terrain.

Finding tracks here is not surprising.

Finding *perfect* tracks here is.

Paradise Lake Close-Range Encounter (135-12)

Face-to-face with something huge

Near Paradise Lake, a couple encountered a Sasquatch at extremely close range.

The creature:

- rose from a log
- turned toward them
- made eye contact
- stood calmly
- then walked away

Eye contact is rare.
Calmness is rarer still.

This creature was curious, not threatened.
It chose to leave.

For me, that is intelligence—not instinct.

Estaire Boulder-Throwing Incident (137-12)

One of the most aggressive encounters in Sudbury history

Two anglers near Estaire were fishing after dark when huge boulders — not stones — began landing in the water near them.

Thrown.
Not rolled.
Not dropped.

Then a massive log blocked their exit trail shortly afterward.

This is:

- intimidation

- boundary enforcement

- territorial display

- deliberate behaviour

Sudbury has more rock-throwing cases than any region in Ontario.

That alone should tell you something.

Mowat Area — Long-Term Cabin Encounters (2008–Present)

Years of visits, pacing, and nighttime activity

A family with a remote cabin near Mowat has experienced:

- pacing
- screaming
- knocking
- handprints on cabin walls
- large shapes moving in the treeline
- long-term repeated visits

This is one of the only multi-year, multi-witness encounter clusters in the Sudbury region.

When a creature returns to the same cabin year after year, it means one thing:

Territory.

Sudbury's creatures do not drift randomly.
They anchor themselves.

The Pattern Revealed

When you map all Sudbury-area sightings, something becomes clear:

This is a superhighway.

Creatures move from:

- Temagami → Sudbury → Lake Superior

- North Bay → Sudbury → Cartier
- Trout Lake → Sudbury → Burwash

Sudbury is the centre point of all of it.

This explains:

- the high number of sightings
- the diversity of behaviours
- the long-term cabin encounters
- the trackways
- the vocalizations
- the road crossings

Sudbury isn't just active.
It is *strategic*.

Everything leads through here.

What Sudbury Has Taught Me

Of all the regions I've explored, Sudbury has taught me some of the most important lessons:

1. These creatures are territorial.

They warn before they act.

2. They revisit locations yearly.

Trout Lake and Mowat prove this.

3. Sudbury is a travel corridor.

A crossroads for movement.

4. Behaviour is consistent.

Rock throwing, pacing, observation.

5. Intelligence is undeniable.

The Estaire and Burwash cases show strategic behaviour.

6. Sudbury's creatures are bold.

Approaching cabins.
Crossing highways.
Standing near towns.

This is not an animal trying to survive.
This is an animal trying to remain unseen—but not always unobservant.

Sudbury creatures are aware.
Alert.
Territorial.
Present.

This is the crossroads of the mystery.

And from here, the trail leads east.

CHAPTER 4 — NORTH BAY: THE EDGE OF THE UNKNOWN

North Bay sits at an interesting point on the map—close enough to southern Ontario to feel familiar, but just far enough north that the land begins to change. The forests tighten. The lakes deepen. The ridges rise. And somewhere between the highways and the old portage routes, the wilderness starts to behave differently.

For years, I used to think of North Bay as a quiet, transitional zone—a place you simply drove through on your way to deeper country. But time, distance, and dozens of reports have taught me otherwise.

North Bay is not a transition.
It's a boundary.
A threshold.
A place where the wild pushes right up against human settlement and doesn't hesitate to cross the line.

And the creatures reported here—whatever they are—seem far more comfortable closing that distance than in many other regions of Ontario.

Sudbury may be the crossroads.
Temagami may be the heart.
But North Bay is the front line.

This chapter explores why.

North Bay's Landscape: A Perfect Convergence Zone

Before diving into the sightings themselves, it's important to understand why North Bay produces the type of encounters it does.

This region contains:

- the vast Duchesnay Falls watershed
- deep, narrow lakes like Trout, Talon, and McQuaby
- dense cedar and pine forest
- ridges that funnel movement
- abandoned logging roads
- old trapline corridors
- wetlands thick enough to swallow a pickup

It is a landscape built for concealment.

Animals move easily through these valleys. Sound carries strangely. Visibility drops to nothing in seconds. And even the most experienced hunters lose their bearings here if they aren't careful.

If a large, silent, intelligent primate lived in Ontario, this is one of the first places it could do so without difficulty.

And the sightings reflect that perfectly.

2015 — The Horseback Encounter

A Sasquatch spooks horses near North Bay

One of the most significant encounters in the area occurred in October 2015, when riders on a trail near North Bay had their horses suddenly panic, freeze, and then attempt to bolt.

Horses don't lie.
Horses don't exaggerate.
Horses react.

The riders reported:

- an enormous dark figure stepping out from the woods

- a sweep of movement that made no sound

- a shape too tall and upright to be a bear

- a strong, musky odour

- total silence after the figure disappeared

One rider said, "The forest felt wrong—like something big was close, but we couldn't see it."

Animals react instinctively to predators.
They reacted that day to something much more than a shadow.

This case marks the beginning of a multi-year pattern.

2014 — The Duchesnay Falls Face in the Trees

A chilling moment caught on camera

In 2014, a witness exploring the forest near Duchesnay Falls captured a photograph that has circulated quietly among researchers: a face peeking through the trees.

Features described include:

- deep-set dark eyes
- a broad, heavy brow
- a forward-sloping forehead
- dark skin or hair
- no visible whites of the eyes

The witness didn't notice the face until reviewing the photo at home.
This is common—creatures that watch hikers, campers, and hunters from cover rarely reveal their full form.

This was observation.
Pure, silent, deliberate observation.

Duchesnay Falls has long been considered one of North Bay's most active micro-regions—and this sighting supports that.

2014 — The Red Eyes on McConnell Lake Road

When curiosity watches from the treeline

McConnell Lake Road has produced some of the most unsettling nighttime encounters in the district.

In August 2014, hikers noticed red eyeshine peering from behind a tree.
Not amber.
Not yellow.
Not green, like a deer or bear.

Red.

The eyes were:

- high—well over 6 feet
- set wide apart
- motionless
- focused

Red eyeshine is rare, and typically associated with animals with a specific reflective layer behind the retina. In Bigfoot research, red eyeshine is a recurring theme in regions with dense evergreen canopy.

This sighting marked a shift:
Not just movement.
Not just sound.
Direct visual contact—even if brief.

North Bay was no longer passive.
It was interacting.

2015 — Corbeil Prints and Vocals

A cluster of activity that drew serious attention

In early 2015, Corbeil saw a spike in reports:

- large, deep tracks found in snow
- long, resonant vocalizations at night
- heavy footsteps circling a rural property
- a strange, rhythmic knocking sound

Two separate investigators visited the site to examine prints:

- midfoot pressure consistent with primate anatomy
- toe splay
- no arch ridge
- consistent stride spacing
- very clear depth compared to surrounding snow

The homeowner described a feeling of being watched for months, especially in winter.

This was not a single encounter.
It was a presence.

2010 — The Father and Son Sighting

A creature steps out during a hunt

Sometime in the summer of 2010, a father and his adult son were hunting in the Nipissing district when a large figure crossed their line of sight.

Both witnesses described:

- height between 7–8 feet
- a wide, muscular upper body
- arms hanging lower than a man's
- a heavy stride
- dark, uniform coloration

This case is important because:

1. It occurred in daylight
2. Both witnesses were experienced outdoorsmen
3. They were familiar with bears and large mammals
4. Their descriptions matched other area reports

This was no misidentification.
This was clarity.

2014 — Larder Lake Tree Snaps

The forest speaks with broken wood

Although technically northeast of North Bay, the Larder Lake 2014 snaps fall within the same movement corridor.

Witnesses found:

- freshly snapped trees

- breaks 7–9 feet off the ground
- no wind damage
- no evidence of machinery
- patterns consistent with primate territorial markers

Tree snapping is not subtle.
It's communication.
It's warning.
It's presence.

And this cluster was large enough to indicate multiple individuals — or prolonged activity.

2013 — The High-Pitched Sounds Near North Bay

One woman in 2013 reported hearing high-pitched sounds, rising and falling in controlled intervals. These were not fox screams. Not coyote yips.

She said, "It sounded like something trying to talk in a language I didn't understand."

The cadence of these sounds mirrors reports from:

- the Sierra Nevada
- the Washington Cascades
- the Great Smoky Mountains

- northern Alberta

This suggests intelligence—not random noise.

2014 — Astorville Vocals (Case 184-14)

A call carried across cold air

In Astorville, long, rolling vocals were heard echoing across frozen lakes. The witness described them as "felt in my chest, not my ears."

Cold air amplifies sound.
Whatever called that night had a chest size far beyond a wolf or moose.

This case pairs perfectly with Corbeil's 2015 activity.

2014 — Bassy Lake Stump That Stood Up

The creature that wasn't a stump at all

A trapper spotted what he thought was a tree stump—until it stood up and ran.

He described:

- a black, massive torso
- long arms

- a forward lean
- powerful strides
- no sound of twigs snapping

Stump sightings are extremely common in areas where the creature remains motionless until discovered.

Bassy Lake proved it again.

Why So Many Encounters Cluster Around North Bay

Mapping the sightings reveals an unmistakable flow:

Temagami → North Bay → Algonquin
and
Sudbury → North Bay → Mattawa / Deep River

North Bay is the eastern gateway for movement across central Ontario.

Reasons:

1. Water Corridors

Rivers and lakes form natural pathways:

- Duchesnay Creek
- Trout Lake

- Four Mile Lake
- the Mattawa River system

2. Ridges and Valleys

The Canadian Shield creates:

- choke points
- funnels
- blind zones
- protected travel corridors

3. Low Human Density Outside Town Limits

Ten minutes outside the city, the world empties.

4. Seasonal Food Abundance

Berries, fish, moose, deer, beaver, roots, grubs—ideal for a large omnivore.

5. Winter Access Routes

Frozen lakes become highways.

North Bay is not just habitat.
It is infrastructure.

The Behavior of the North Bay Creature

Across all sightings, patterns emerge:

1. Observation From Cover

Duchesnay Falls
McConnell Lake
Astorville

2. Road and Trail Crossings

Father and son encounter
Bassy Lake "stump" incident

3. Close Proximity Without Contact

Horseback encounter
Corbeil prints
Vocalizations near homes

4. Strong Vocal Presence

Astorville
North Bay high-pitched anomaly
Larder Lake snaps

5. Winter Boldness

Corbeil
Duchesnay Falls
Horseback encounter

This creature—whatever it is—seems more willing to approach human activity in North Bay than in other regions.

Not aggressively.
Just… curiously.

What North Bay Has Taught Me

North Bay taught me something important about this mystery:

The creature is not afraid of people.
It is cautious, observant, and calculating, but not terrified.

And that matters.

Temagami's creature keeps distance.
Sudbury's warns.
Algonquin's watches.

But North Bay's approaches.

It watches families on horseback.
It circles rural properties.
It stands behind thin rows of trees near a waterfall.
It crosses roads in daylight.
It leaves prints practically at the edge of town.

If I had to guess, I'd say North Bay is not just a travel corridor—
it is a testing ground.

A place where the creatures gauge humans.
A place where they learn our patterns.
A place where the line between our world and theirs gets thinner.

North Bay is the edge of something.
The edge of the unknown.

The edge of understanding.
The edge of a boundary neither we nor the creatures fully see.

This is a region where the forest doesn't just watch.
It evaluates.

And that tells me one thing:

The creature in North Bay is not just passing through.

It lives here.
Moves here.
Listens here.
And on certain nights—
when the wind is right and the branches are still—
it reveals itself.

Not fully.
Not brazenly.
But just enough to let you know the truth:

Something walks the forests of North Bay.

And it knows you're here too.

CHAPTER 5 — COCHRANE: GATEWAY TO THE JAMES BAY WILDERNESS

There's a moment when you leave the last gas station south of Cochrane and head north on Highway 11 where the land begins to stretch in a different way. It's not like the forests around North Bay or the high ridges of Temagami. It's something far older, far wider, and far more unforgiving.

The trees thin.
The sky expands.
And everything ahead of you feels like an endless horizon of muskeg, black spruce, and silence.

This is not a region you simply travel through.
This is a frontier.
The beginning of the James Bay wilderness.
A place where people are rare and the land dominates everything.

Cochrane and its surrounding districts have produced some of Ontario's strangest, boldest, and most revealing Sasquatch encounters—sightings that hint at something bigger, stronger, and more fearless than the creatures seen farther south.

If Sudbury is the crossroads,
and North Bay is the threshold,
then Cochrane is the northern gateway—
a borderland where the mystery grows larger, louder, and harder to ignore.

The Cochrane Wilderness: A Creature's Perfect Domain

To understand the sightings here, you must understand the land itself.

This region is:

- vast
- wet
- flat
- heavily forested
- almost impossible to navigate without river routes
- sparsely populated
- geographically connected to the Hudson Bay Lowlands

It's territory where large animals vanish without a trace.
Where sound travels strangely.
Where winter lasts half the year.
Where even experienced hunters feel small.

If a creature wanted space to roam unseen,
this would be the place.

And the encounters recorded here—especially those involving multiple individuals—suggest something far more complex than isolated wanderers.

This is not a stray animal.
This is a population.

October 1992 — The Policeman's Nighttime Encounter

A Cochrane legend that still holds weight

One of the most famous Cochrane encounters occurred along the Trans-Canada Highway, about 100 miles west of the town.

A police officer driving at night saw a large, upright figure cross the highway in front of him. His description remains one of the clearest from the region:

- towering height
- a smooth, purposeful stride
- shoulders wider than a human's
- a thick, uniform body shape
- long arms swinging naturally
- no hesitation, no fear

He immediately filed a report—an unusual step for law enforcement at the time.

The location matters:

The Trans-Canada at that point is surrounded by endless forest and muskeg. Nothing lives out there except bears, wolves, moose… and something else.

Sightings by officers carry weight.
This one never faded from local memory.

And it wasn't the last.

South Porcupine — The Creature in the Headlights (Multiple Years)

Multiple reports, same region, same behaviour

The South Porcupine area east of Timmins is one of the strangest hotspots in the region. Multiple encounters occurred here over decades, each disturbingly similar.

2015 — The Night Roadcrossing

A driver traveling near South Porcupine saw a "tall, black, very wide figure" illuminated in their headlights as it crossed the road.

It didn't run.
It didn't panic.
It just stepped across the asphalt with long, fluid strides and disappeared into the trees.

1961 — The Raspberry Cane Incident

In August 1961—one of the earliest documented Cochrane-area cases—a creature parted raspberry canes and peeked out at a witness.

The details match modern sightings:

- dark face

- long fingers

- deliberate, slow movement

- no sound

- intelligent observation

These behaviours span 54 years.

Same region.
Same patterns.
Same creature profile.

When sightings repeat across decades, you're not dealing with mistakes.
You're dealing with territory.

Spring 2013 — The Four-Male Encounter Near Moosonee

One of the most shocking multi-creature sightings in Ontario history

This case demands attention.

In 2013, hunters northwest of Moosonee—deep in the muskeg between Kashachewan and the river systems—saw something almost no one expects:

Four male Sasquatch walking in single file out of the water.

Not one.
Not two.
Four.

Descriptions include:

- all were tall and muscular
- hair varying in shade from black to dark brown
- similar body proportions
- moving with remarkable grace
- completely silent
- aware of the witnesses but not threatened

The men who witnessed this have never come forward publicly. They have allowed researchers to speak on their behalf, but only to a limited degree.

Their reason?

"These are real animals.
They don't want trouble with people."

This sighting implies:

- a family group
- coordinated movement
- possible migration routes
- presence far into the James Bay Lowlands

And it reinforces one of my strongest beliefs:

Ontario's Bigfoot population is not solitary. It is structured.

2012 — Larder Lake Tree Snaps (Case 195-15)

A trail of broken trees stretching deep into the bush

Although geographically overlapping with North Bay's east end, the Larder Lake region also feeds north into Cochrane and Timmins.

In 2012, a series of freshly snapped trees—some up to 9 feet off the ground—were found in a concentrated area.

Features:

- breaks were clean
- wood twisted before snapping
- multiple trunks in a row
- no machinery tracks
- no storm damage

Tree snapping on this scale is:

- territorial
- communicative
- indicative of size and strength

And the clustering matched other primate-like territorial markers documented worldwide.

October 2012 — Iroquois Falls Scream

A response that wasn't supposed to exist

Two moose hunters north of Iroquois Falls gave a cow call shortly after sunset.

Seconds later, something answered.

Not a bull.
Not a bear.
Not a coyote.

Something huge screamed back, then snapped large branches.

Hunters know the sound of a bull moose.
They know how moose crash through brush.
They know vocalization patterns.

This was different.

The scream was:

- deeper
- longer
- more resonant
- almost human

- undeniably powerful

This wasn't a misidentification.
This was communication.

And it wasn't friendly.

The Cochrane Pattern: Roadways, Rivers, and Remote Land

When all the sightings are mapped, a clear pattern emerges.

The encounters cluster along:

- the Trans-Canada Highway
- old logging and mining corridors
- the river systems feeding toward James Bay
- the muskeg routes between Cochrane, Moosonee, and Timmins
- the dense boreal forest east and west of Highway 11

Creatures here move along predictable geographic features:

1. Waterways

The rivers around Cochrane and Moosonee form natural travel corridors.

2. Road Edges

Nighttime crossings on 101 and 11 match global Bigfoot roadcrossing behaviour.

3. Muskeg Plateaus

Soft ground preserves tracks but also makes movement easier for large-footed animals.

4. Sparse Population

There are fewer eyes, fewer roads, fewer lights.

5. Winter Access

Frozen muskeg becomes an open highway for months.

This region is not just habitat.
It is freedom—uninterrupted space for something large and intelligent to roam without interference.

Behaviour in the Cochrane District

Comparing all encounters reveals unique traits:

1. Bold, Close-Range Encounters

The policeman
South Porcupine
Iroquois Falls

These creatures don't avoid roads. They cross them confidently.

2. Multi-Individual Sightings

The Moosonee four-male sighting
One of the rarest encounter types in Ontario.

3. Vocal Responses to Human Calls

Hunters receiving direct answers.
That does not happen with bears or moose.

4. Observation Without Fear

Peeking from cane patches
Standing in headlights
Crossing slowly and deliberately

5. Deep Territorial Marking

Tree snaps
Branch breaks
Multi-area clusters

Cochrane's creature is not timid, not panicked, and not merely passing through.

It is established.

And in some places—dominant.

Why Cochrane Matters More Than People Realize

Most people don't think of Cochrane when they think of wilderness mysteries.
They think of Temagami, Algonquin, Sudbury, or the Pacific Northwest.

But Cochrane holds something the others do not:

1. Access to the Largest Intact Wilderness in Ontario

The James Bay Lowlands stretch farther than the eye can comprehend.

2. Active First Nations Knowledge

Many experiences remain unreported, shared only within communities.

3. Population Clusters That Allow Bold Approaches

South Porcupine
Timmins outskirts
Remote roads

4. Road Networks That Cut Through Prime Habitat

Highways attract crossing behaviour.

5. Seasonal Animal Migrations

Moose
Caribou
Beaver
Bear
All abundant.

This region is not an edge.
It is a beginning—the start of a land so vast and so little traveled that a population of large, elusive primates could live undetected for centuries.

And based on the evidence, they have.

What Cochrane Has Taught Me

Every region in Ontario reveals a different truth.

Temagami teaches caution.
Sudbury teaches territory.
North Bay teaches curiosity.

But Cochrane?
Cochrane teaches scale.

This region reveals:

- these creatures are not isolated

- they may travel in groups

- they have territory that spans enormous distances

- they respond to human calls

- they approach roads, cabins, and hunters

- they survive easily in harsh northern environments

- they move farther north than many people realize

Cochrane is where the mystery stops being a question
and becomes a system.

A living, breathing system of movement, behaviour, territory, and population.

This is a land built for giants—
and every account, from the policeman on the highway to the hunters who saw four males emerge from the water, points to the same conclusion:

Something lives in the Cochrane district.
Something big.
Something intelligent.
Something that has been here far longer than we have.

And the deeper north you go,
the closer you get to the truth.

CHAPTER 6 — KENORA: SHADOWS ON THE WATER

Kenora is a place where land and water blur together.
Where islands stretch toward the horizon like stepping stones into the unknown.
Where the wind carries sound in ways you can't predict.
Where the night settles fast and absolute.

If Sudbury is a crossroads
and Cochrane is a frontier,
then Kenora is a labyrinth—a maze of lakes, bays, inlets, old growth, traplines, island chains, and waterways so complex that even seasoned locals get turned around.

And it's here, in this vast watery wilderness, that some of Ontario's most unsettling reports have surfaced. Not one or two. Not scattered. But a history—a tapestry of sightings that stretches across centuries, cultures, communities, and geography.

Kenora holds secrets.
It holds stories.
And out on those dark lakes, it holds something else:

A presence that moves like a shadow between the islands.

Kenora's Wilderness: A Creature's Perfect Domain

To understand why so much activity happens here, you have to understand the land — or rather, the *water*, because water dominates everything.

Lake of the Woods alone has:

- 14,552 islands
- over 65,000 miles of shoreline (more than Lake Superior)
- cliffs, caves, remote inlets, marsh belts, untouched forests
- First Nations land rarely visited by outsiders
- massive stretches of unoccupied wilderness

No region in Ontario offers this degree of concealment.
A creature could cross the region without ever touching the same island twice.

Movement here is not linear.
It's fluid, shifting with seasons, food availability, and territory.

Every researcher who studies the region comes to the same conclusion:

If Bigfoot exists in Ontario, Lake of the Woods is the strongest candidate for sustained long-term habitation.

And the encounters bear that out.

2022–Present — The Fort Hope Sightings

Two creatures. Tracks. Photos. Video. Repeated encounters.

One of the most significant modern developments in Ontario Bigfoot research is happening north of Kenora, near Fort Hope and the remote communities surrounding it.

Multiple witnesses — from hunters to river travelers to community members — have reported:

- two large Bigfoot individuals traveling together
- broad daylight sightings
- tracks photographed in snow, mud, and moss
- video footage of a trackway
- a still photograph of one of the creatures

Descriptions were consistent:

- extremely large
- dark brown or black
- wide-shouldered
- long-armed
- moving smoothly through dense bush

What sets these sightings apart is not just the clarity — but the consistency.

These encounters span multiple months and multiple observers, across an area where:

- moose populations are high
- human presence is low

- river systems connect vast distances
- winter tracks remain preserved for days

The Fort Hope pair may be part of a small family group that ranges across the Kenora district and into northern First Nations territories.

It's not just a sighting cluster.
It's a population indicator.

2009 — The Sioux Narrows Bear Carcass Incident

One of the strangest thefts ever reported

In 2009, workers at a tourist camp near Sioux Narrows reported to have had a bear carcass stolen from in between the cabins that had been left overnight. No Drag marks or disturbance of any kind.

This was not a rumor.
Multiple workers witnessed different events throughout the summer:

- something tall moving between cabins at night
- a shadowy figure carrying the bear carcass
- heavy, bipedal footsteps
- deep growls
- the distinct feeling of being watched for nights afterward

A bear carcass is not easy to carry.
Not for a human.
Not for a hoaxer.

The workers described the creature as:

- upright
- at least 7 feet tall
- dark
- silent except for heavy breathing

It vanished into the bush without a struggle.

This event alone is one of the most compelling behavioral clues in the entire region.

August 2006 — The Daylight Sioux Narrows Sighting

Clear visual, perfect conditions, multiple witnesses

Only a few years before the carcass theft, a daylight sighting occurred near the same area.

Witnesses described:

- an enormous dark figure
- long arms swinging naturally
- fluid movement

- no hesitation
- a non-bear gait
- a creature much wider than a human

Three elements matter here:

1. Daylight
2. Multiple witnesses
3. Same region as the 2009 incidents

When sightings cluster this tightly in geography and behaviour, you're no longer dealing with coincidence.

You're dealing with territory.

And Sioux Narrows is territory rich with inaccessible forest and hidden movement corridors.

June 1998 — The Sioux Lookout Fisherman Encounter

Up the waterway, early morning, unexpected movement

A fisherman boating up a narrow waterway near Sioux Lookout spotted a tall, upright figure step out onto the shoreline.

He watched it for several seconds as it looked toward the boat, then turned and walked into the trees.

Important details:

- the figure was not startled
- it did not run
- it moved with calm confidence
- it showed no interest in hiding

This is consistent with a creature accustomed to the area — not passing through.

2013 — Kenora Campground Vocalizations

A couple camping near Kenora reported hearing:

- long, resonant howls
- rhythmic knocking
- strange distant wails that rose and fell

They described the atmosphere as "dead silent afterward" — a classic sign of predator-level movement.

And the sounds matched:

- Pacific Northwest vocal patterns
- Minnesota "whoop" recordings
- classic Sasquatch howl cadence

Kenora's creatures are vocal.
Very vocal.

2014 — Dinorwic Vocals (183-14)

In 2014, in the Dinorwic region east of Dryden, witnesses described:

- powerful, echoing vocalizations
- rising howls with chest-deep resonance
- nighttime calls unlike wolves or coyotes

Dinorwic is swamp country — thick cover, floating mats, and ancient spruce. Perfect ground for anything that wants silence and concealment.

This case reinforced a pattern:

Kenora-class creatures speak across distance.

They don't just grunt or knock.
They *announce*.

February 20, 1987 — The Red Gut Bay Face-to-Face Encounter

One of the earliest modern era Class A sightings

A trapper near Sioux Lookout encountered a Sasquatch face-to-face on his trapline.

This case remains one of the most chilling in the region because:

- it was close
- the witness was experienced
- the creature was calm
- there was no misidentification

Descriptions include:

- tall, massively built
- dark fur
- broad, flat face
- deep-set eyes
- long arms
- silent, slow departure

The trapper abandoned his line for weeks afterward.

This encounter confirms a behavioural theme:

Kenora's creatures are not afraid of humans.
They are aware, curious, and confident.

2008 — Grassy Narrows Blueberry Pickers Encounter

Height, footprint, and a rare six-toed anomaly

In Grassy Narrows, several First Nations witnesses encountered a tall, skinny Bigfoot while blueberry picking.

Details:

- estimated height of eight feet
- long, narrow body type
- upright posture
- dark hair
- a massive six-toed footprint found near a beaver pond

A plaster cast was made and shipped for examination.

Why this matters:

Six-toed Bigfoot reports appear in:

- the Pacific Northwest
- Alaska
- British Columbia
- parts of Manitoba
- and now, Kenora

It suggests genetic variation within a population — or a specific lineage.

This is the kind of detail hoaxers never think to include.

2006 — The Snelgrove Lake Case

One of Ontario's most famous encounters

The Snelgrove Lake encounter is legendary — so much so that it made its way onto *MonsterQuest TV Series*.

At a remote cabin accessible only by floatplane, a group of fishermen encountered:

- strange nighttime howls
- heavy footsteps
- rhythmic knocking
- objects thrown at the cabin
- large footprints
- rocks hitting the building

Later investigations found:

- deeper prints
- more rock-throwing
- repeated visits to the cabin

Follow-up expeditions produced similar results.

Snelgrove is a perfect example of:

- territorial behaviour
- curiosity about human structures

- nighttime dominance display

And it sits squarely within the Kenora district's northern wilderness.

1996 — Lac Seul Firefighters Find a Track

A footprint photographed during a forest fire operation

Firefighters battling a wildfire near Lac Seul found:

- a large barefoot track in dried mud
- photographed next to a tape measure
- deep heel impression
- clear toe definition

The location was remote — a place where no humans should have been walking barefoot.

This is one of the oldest photographically documented tracks in the Kenora region.

1993–94 — The Red Gut Bay Teenage Hunter Incident

A massive creature crosses the trail in seconds

Near Rainy Lake, a 14-year-old grouse hunter encountered a huge creature that stepped across the trail in only a few strides.

He described being:

- frozen
- terrified
- unable to process the size
- unable to return to the area

Teenagers often panic during bear encounters — but they don't describe upright, long-striding creatures.

This was something else.

Longlac — Tracks and Feces (132-12)

A biological clue rare in Ontario

Hunters near Longlac found:

- multiple tracks in mud and sand
- large piles of feces
- prints arranged in a clear trackway
- photos documenting everything

The feces sample was analyzed and determined to be:

non-human primate in structure
(based on consistency and foot placement evidence).

This is not proof — but it is *biological direction*.

Why the Kenora Region Is So Active

When you map every sighting, every vocalization, every track, a pattern becomes undeniable:

Kenora is a population hub.

This region has:

1. Abundant food sources

Moose
Deer
Bear
Fish
Berry patches
Beaver
Roots

2. Unbroken wilderness extending into Manitoba

One of the largest forest systems on the continent.

3. Water routes for silent travel

Sasquatch behaviour globally correlates with water.

4. Extremely low human density

Witnesses are rare — sightings are significant.

5. Island chains perfect for seasonal movement

Predators thrive here.
So would a large primate.

6. Strong First Nations oral history

Reports long pre-dating Western documentation.

Behavioural Patterns Unique to Kenora

Across all the Kenora-area encounters, clear traits emerge:

1. Comfort around water

Many sightings occur near shorelines, rivers, and islands.

2. Bold food acquisition

Stealing a bear carcass is no small feat.

3. Multi-individual movement

Fort Hope and Grassy Narrows suggest families or pairs.

4. Highly vocal interactions

The region has some of the loudest and most powerful calls.

5. Road and camp proximity

Snelgrove and Sioux Narrows events show familiarity with human structures.

6. Upright confidence

Most creatures walked calmly, not fleeing.

This is not a creature hiding in desperation.
It's a creature living comfortably in its environment.

What Kenora Has Taught Me

Kenora taught me that Ontario's forests are deeper than we think.
Darker than we imagine.
More alive than most people will ever realize.

It taught me that:

- these creatures are not solitary wanderers
- they move in pairs
- they may even travel in groups
- they use water as highways
- they do not fear the night
- they do not fear the cold
- and they do not fear us

But they stay hidden.

Not because they are weak —
but because they are strong enough to choose when they want to be seen.

Kenora is the region where the mystery becomes undeniable.
Where the shadows between the islands feel aware.
Where sound carries further than it should.
Where movement on the shoreline catches your eye at dusk.
Where a shape steps between the pines and leaves no trace but memory.

This is the lake country of giants.

And their shadows still move across the water.

CHAPTER 7 — THUNDER BAY: THE STORM COAST

Thunder Bay is a region that feels carved by something ancient—wind, water, ice, and maybe something else entirely. The land here is harsher, rougher, more exposed. Storms roll off Lake Superior with a force that belongs to a different world. Black spruce bends in wind that has blown uninterrupted for hundreds of miles. Waves smash against cliffs that rise like broken teeth from the water.

Everything in Thunder Bay is bigger.
Darker.
Heavier.

If Kenora is the land of shadows on the water, then Thunder Bay is a place where shadows walk the shore.

For decades, locals have whispered about strange sightings in the ravines, the old logging roads, the far-north rivers, and the flats where the boreal forest squeezes tight against the largest freshwater lake on Earth. And those sightings aren't small. They're physical. Vocal. Territorial.

Thunder Bay doesn't just hint at Bigfoot.
Thunder Bay warns you.

This is a region where animals grow large, storms grow violent, and something—whatever it is—seems to move with the confidence of a long-established apex predator.

Let's start with one of the most unsettling cases on Lake Superior.

August 2005 — "Something's Throwing Rocks at Us"

North of Thunder Bay — a boating trip turns into a confrontation

In August 2005, a group of boaters travelled along the rugged shoreline north of Thunder Bay—sharp cliffs, deep water, old forests clinging to rock. It's a place where cabins stand alone for miles, and where shoreline access is limited to those with boats and knowledge of the lake.

As they approached a narrow inlet, rocks began hitting the water near their boat.

Not pebbles.
Not falling debris.
Thrown rocks.

The witnesses reported:

- splashes large enough to send spray over the side
- rocks landing with clear trajectory
- repeated throws
- no visible people
- dense forest right up to the waterline
- complete silence between impacts

The rocks did not drop from cliffs—there were none above them. They came laterally, from inside the treeline.

There are only three animals in Ontario capable of throwing objects:

- humans
- raccoons (but not heavy rocks)
- primates

And Thunder Bay does not have raccoons that bench press granite.

This encounter mirrors classic Pacific Northwest Sasquatch behaviour:

- warn first, reveal later
- control territory through intimidation
- avoid direct sightlines
- maintain dominance at a distance

Thunder Bay's northern coast is vast, sparsely inhabited, and difficult to navigate.
Whatever threw those rocks was comfortable enough to assert itself—and confident enough to know the humans were outmatched.

December 1958 — Tracks Across a Snowy Field

Thunder Bay's oldest recorded case still carries weight

Long before Bigfoot became a cultural phenomenon, something crossed a snow-covered field near Thunder Bay in the winter of 1958.

Farm owners found:

- a line of large, bipedal tracks

- each print longer than a human foot

- no drag marks

- no sign of machinery

- an extremely long stride

- tracks heading straight into forest too thick for a person to walk through

No one reported sightings in that era—just evidence.
Clean, precise, and preserved in early winter snow.

This case matters for one reason:

It predates media influence.
There was no description template, no online hoaxing culture, no Bigfoot TV shows.

The evidence existed before the story.

And in mystery work, that's significant.

2014 — Whitesand River Vocalizations

Voices in the valley no person could produce

The Whitesand River cuts through a remote stretch of the Thunder Bay region—miles north of the city, surrounded by thick spruce and swamp. In 2014, a witness heard striking vocalizations at night:

- deep

- powerful

- long, rising howls

- followed by grunts and chest-low moans

These were not wolves.
Local hunters confirm wolves have a distinct, chorus-like rise and fall.
These calls were solitary... and huge.

The witness described the howls as:
"Something with lungs twice the size of a man."

What makes this case even more compelling is that Whitesand River is part of a natural movement corridor leading:

- west toward Dryden

- north into unpopulated bush

- and south toward the Lake Superior highlands

This region acts as a tributary system—not just for water, but for wildlife.

Large predators travel this corridor.
And something larger seems to travel it too.

Case 141-12 — Tree Snaps and Unknown Scat, West of Thunder Bay

A biological clue in an otherwise silent forest

A witness walking through his father's property west of Thunder Bay came across:

- tree snaps 7 feet off the ground
- fresh, clean breaks
- multiple snapped trees in a pattern
- a pile of unknown scat nearby

Tree snaps that high are not:

- moose
- bear
- wind
- snow load

They are deliberate.
Placed.
Communicative.

For primates—especially large ones—tree snapping is territorial:

- warnings

- boundary setting
- navigation marking
- family communication

The scat found nearby was described as:

- large
- dense
- fibrous
- unlike any local predator
- too big for wolf or cougar
- not consistent with bear

Biological evidence in Ontario is rare.
This case stands out.

Case 179-14 — Whitesand River Sighting

A creature steps into view—then vanishes without sound

Around the same area as the vocalizations, a witness observed a tall, dark figure standing partially concealed by spruce.

Details:

- upright silhouette
- long arm

- massive torso

- no sound as it moved

- disappeared behind a rock outcrop

Thunder Bay sightings repeatedly note silent movement.

Large humans do not move silently through spruce deadfall.
Bears do not walk upright smoothly.
Moose do not hide behind trees at head height.

This was something different.

2019 — Dryden Family Records Vocals

A recording that still circulates among researchers

Technically closer to the Thunder Bay division than Kenora, the Dryden area has long been part of the same wilderness corridor. In 2019, a family recorded:

- loud, sustained, bellowing calls

- coming from the treeline

- late evening

- spaced in consistent intervals

- no animal match found

Multiple experts informally reviewed the audio.
Consensus:

Not wolf.
Not moose.
Not human.
Deep chest resonance.
Primate-like projection.

The recording became one of the most important modern vocal captures in Ontario.

Thunder Bay's Unique Geography: Why This Region Behaves Differently

Thunder Bay is both a shield and a trap.

1. The Lake Superior Effect

Wind, pressure systems, and rolling storm fronts create a soundscape unlike anywhere else.

Calls carry far.
Knocks echo.
And movement can be heard at great distance.

2. Rugged Escarpments

Sheer cliffs and ravines create natural hideouts and vantage points.

3. Vast, Unbroken Forest

Between Thunder Bay and Sioux Lookout lies one of the largest stretches of uninterrupted forest in Ontario.

4. Sparse Settlements

Cabins exist—but miles apart.

5. Prey Abundance

Moose country.
Deer.
Beaver.
Fish in unbelievable supply.

6. Travel Corridors

The Whitesand and Kaministiquia river systems act as north-south highways for wildlife.

This region is perfect habitat for a large, elusive, intelligent primate.

Not good—perfect.

Behavioural Patterns in Thunder Bay

Reviewing every case reveals several consistent traits:

1. Rock Throwing

The 2005 boat encounter mirrors classic intimidation behaviour.

2. High Vantage Observation

Multiple sightings occur near cliffs, ravines, and hilltops.

3. Powerful Vocalizations

Thunder Bay creatures call more often—and with more force—than those in Sudbury or North Bay.

4. Silent Retreat

Creatures vanish without sound, even in dense underbrush.

5. Confidence Around Humans

Crossings
Camp proximity
Approaching boats
Unintimidated vocal displays

Thunder Bay Sasquatch are not shy.

Historic First Nations Knowledge

Long before European settlement, the Ojibwe told stories about:

- tall wildmen

- creatures living along Lake Superior's cliffs

- beings that "walked on two legs but spoke like thunder"

- watchers who lived on the edge of the deep woods

These stories cluster along the same regions as modern sightings:

- Whitesand

- Lac des Mille Lacs

- Nipigon corridor

- Lake Superior east shore

Folklore aligns with geography.
Geography aligns with sightings.
Sightings align with behaviour.

That is not random.

What Thunder Bay Has Taught Me

Thunder Bay is where the mystery changes shape.

Not gentle.
Not quiet.
Not distant.

It is:

- bold

- loud

- territorial

- physical

- intentional

The region taught me that:

1. These creatures are capable of strength well beyond human level.

Rock-throwing on large scales is no small feat.

2. They choose confrontation or avoidance depending on context.

3. They move in a way no known animal does — upright, silent, confident.

4. They are not simply passing through — they are established.

5. The northern shorelines of Superior may be one of the last great refuges for them.

Thunder Bay's encounters feel older, deeper, more primal than the rest of Ontario.
Something about the land demands respect — and so does whatever walks within it.

When you stand on the Superior shoreline at dusk, watching waves crash against ancient rock, you understand something:

The land here remembers things.
And one of those things still walks the forest.

CHAPTER 8 — SAULT STE. MARIE: THE GATEWAY TO THE GREAT UNKNOWN

There are regions in Ontario that feel wild, and then there are regions that feel *unfamiliar*.
The Algoma District — stretching from Sault Ste. Marie up along the north shore of Lake Superior — belongs to the latter.

This is not gentle wilderness.
This is not the soft, pine-lined quiet of Muskoka.
This is country shaped by water, stone, storms, and old forces that don't care who you are.

Algoma is fierce.
Raw.
Untamed in a way most people will never experience.

And the strange thing about this place — the unsettling thing — is that nearly every witness who's seen or heard something unusual here describes the exact same feeling:

"We were not alone."

That sensation threads through every report, from Old Woman Bay to Searchmont to Lake Superior Provincial Park. A feeling of presence. Not friendly. Not hostile. Just *aware*.

If the Thunder Bay chapter was the coastline of power,
then Sault Ste. Marie is the threshold of something older and far more watchful.

Let's start with the sound that still bothers people decades later.

August 2004 — Whistles in the Night

North of Sault Ste. Marie — the forest that answered back

Two campers set up for the evening north of the Soo, miles down a logging road with no other vehicles, no other camps, nothing but trees and silence.

Around midnight, they heard:

- a sharp whistle
- then another
- then a third
- all from different directions
- all identical

Coyotes don't whistle.
Owls don't whistle like that.
Humans don't whistle in perfect mimicry from three sides of a camp in the middle of nowhere.

The witnesses said the hair on their arms stood up instantly.
One of them whispered:
"It's communicating."

What unsettled them wasn't the whistle itself —
it was the *response*.
Something else answered from behind the treeline.

The forest was speaking that night.

And they were caught in the middle of the conversation.

September 2004 — Rock-Throwing, Lake Superior Provincial Park

Something didn't want them there

Only weeks after the whistle incident, a family fishing inside Lake Superior Provincial Park heard splashes behind them.

Then heavy rocks — not small ones — began landing near their boat.

These weren't falling from cliffs.
They came from shore.
From something standing just a little back from the treeline.

The father described:

- the steady rhythm of throws

- each rock thrown with force

- something large pacing just out of sight

- a feeling of hostility in the air

This wasn't warning behaviour like in Sudbury.
This was territorial aggression, full stop.

Whatever lives in this region doesn't avoid confrontation.
It *initiates* it.

February 29, 2014 — Blue Eyeshine Across the Road (Case 168-14)

The eyes that watched

A witness driving near the Algoma backroads saw two blue points of light staring from across the road.

Blue eyeshine is rare — extremely rare — in Ontario wildlife.
Wolf eyes typically shine amber or yellow.
Moose shine green.
Black bears reflect red or orange.

But this?
Cold, deep, electric blue.

The eyes were:

- too far apart for wolf

- too high off the ground for bear

- too intense to be reflective trash or light artefact

After staring for several seconds, the creature moved —
not downward like a quadruped,
but sideways and upward,
as though standing fully upright.

Then came the sounds:

- heavy branches snapping

- something pacing

- answering snaps from deeper in the woods

Not just one creature.
At least two.

This case is a turning point for Algoma.
It's the moment the region went from "possible activity" to active territory.

Summer 2013 — Searchmont Activity (Case 161-14)

The snowmelt revealed the truth

North of the Soo, in the old logging and ski country around Searchmont, hikers began noticing something odd after the 2014 snowmelt:

- twisted branches
- large tracks in saturated moss
- deep impressions behind a hunting cabin
- broken saplings arranged in unnatural patterns

Activity had been heard the previous summer — knocks, pacing, occasional distant calls — but the land revealed far more when the snow receded.

Some of the prints were enormous:
15 to 17 inches long, long stride spacing, no drag marks.

Snow preserves the truth better than soil.
There's no faking a 17-inch foot in spring snowpack.

Whatever moved through Searchmont wasn't passing through. It lived there.

March 8, 2011 — Old Woman Bay Trackway (Case 109-11)

The most famous track site on the Superior shore

Old Woman Bay is one of the most dramatic locations on Lake Superior — towering cliffs, cold wind, and a shoreline that feels haunted even on sunny days.

During an investigation of a previous road-crossing sighting, researchers found:

- large, crisp tracks in the snow
- a clear, straight trackway
- consistent depth
- wide toes
- no evidence of hoaxing

They followed the tracks until they disappeared into dense brush where no one could easily go without leaving sign.

The Old Woman Bay prints match the anatomy of many others in Ontario:

- midfoot pressure
- flat, non-arched profile

- wide forefoot
- long stride
- anatomically correct toe positions

This trackway—combined with the region's earlier roadcrossing reports—marks Old Woman Bay as a consistent hotspot.

It's one of the few places in Ontario where the land, the sightings, and the evidence all point in the same direction:

Something uses this shoreline regularly.

June 3, 2008 — Elliot Lake Sighting (Case 182-15)

The creature that stepped from the trees

South of the Soo, near Elliot Lake, a witness saw a massive dark figure step out from the forest as they rounded a bend.

Details include:

- towering height
- wide torso
- hair that moved in the wind
- an upright posture
- a silent retreat

Elliot Lake sits at the southern edge of Algoma's deep wilderness — a region full of abandoned mining lands and untouched lake systems.

This sighting confirms that activity isn't limited to Superior's shoreline.
It extends deep inland.

The Algoma Corridor: A Pattern Emerges

When all Sault Ste. Marie–area encounters are mapped, a striking pattern appears:

A continuous corridor of activity from Elliot Lake → Lake Superior Provincial Park → Wawa → Pukaskwa → Thunder Bay.

It's not random.
It's not scattered.
It's a chain.

A living, breathing migration route — or possibly multiple territories belonging to a connected population.

Key characteristics of this region:

1. The Land Is Vertical

Cliffs, ravines, and escarpments create natural hiding and lookout points.

2. Weather Masks Sound

Lake Superior's wind swallows noise, making detection difficult.

3. Food Is Plentiful

Moose
Deer
Caribou
Fish
Berries
Roots
Winterkill carcasses

4. Access Is Limited

Few roads
Fewer people
Many dead-end trails

5. Old-growth pockets remain untouched

Areas that haven't changed in centuries.

This land is perfect for a large, intelligent creature that prefers distance but isn't afraid of proximity.

Behaviour Unique to the Sault Ste. Marie Region

Across all Algoma sightings, the same traits emerge:

1. Whistles

Very rare in Ontario — extremely common in 2004 cases.

2. Rock Throwing

Aggressive, direct, territorial.

3. Eyeshine

The blue eyeshine case is one of the clearest in Ontario history.

4. Snow Trackways

Old Woman Bay
Searchmont
Wawa corridor

5. Multiple Individuals

Branch snaps answering one another.

6. Proximity to Water

Nearly every case occurs along Lake Superior or its tributaries.

What stands out is confidence.

The creatures here don't hide the way they do in Algonquin or North Bay.
They confront.
They watch.
They announce.
They warn.

This is apex-predator territory.
And whatever lives here acts like one.

What Sault Ste. Marie Has Taught Me

This region reveals a truth that other chapters have only hinted at:

Bigfoot in Ontario is not one creature — it's a population.
And populations have territories.

Algoma taught me that:

- these creatures communicate

- they travel in coordinated ways

- they maintain boundaries

- they warn humans when necessary

- they use geography to their advantage

- they are part of a larger system stretching from Lake Superior to James Bay

If Kenora showed intelligence,
and Thunder Bay revealed power,
then Sault Ste. Marie shows organization.

This is land where something old has lived for generations — long before the Soo canal, long before European logging crews, long before highways carved through the trees.

And the truth settles in when you stand on the Superior shore at dusk:

The wind howls, the lake breathes, the pines shift,
and somewhere behind you, just out of view,
the forest watches.

Something walks here.
Something tall.

Something strong.
Something aware.

And in the Sault Ste. Marie region…
it doesn't hide its presence.

It lets you know.

CHAPTER 9 — DURHAM COUNTY: THE EDGE OF THE SOUTHERN WILDERNESS

Durham County is where things start to feel strange in a different way.

It's not the deep wilderness of Temagami.
It's not the storm-carved coast of Thunder Bay.
It's not the raw frontier of Cochrane or the labyrinth of Kenora.

Durham County sits between worlds — caught in a transition zone where Ontario's southern farmland begins to give way to thick cedar swamps, winding ATV trails, forgotten marshlands, and forest pockets that look far bigger on the inside than they do on a map.

People underestimate this region.
They shouldn't.

The encounters here may not be deep-north remote, but they carry something else entirely: proximity, boldness, and behavior that suggests these creatures are comfortable operating much closer to the edges of human settlement.

Durham's forests hide old railway beds, ravines, abandoned farm roads, and long stretches of swamp that most people never visit.

And in those places — the quiet ones, the ones without cell signal, the ones only hunters and off-roaders know — something large moves.

Something that doesn't fear being close.

The Land: A Hidden Corridor

Durham County is deceptive terrain. To outsiders, it looks like:

- rolling farmland
- small forests
- cottage roads
- horse trails
- quiet towns between Lake Ontario and the Kawarthas

But to anyone who knows the land — really knows it — Durham is a lot more than that.

It contains:

- miles of old-growth hardwood hidden behind farmland
- cedar swamps that swallow noise
- dead-end trails miles deep
- creeks and river corridors leading north to Kawartha Lakes
- thick crown land pockets
- huge marsh belts where footprints can remain for days

This region forms a natural wildlife pipeline between:

- the Oak Ridges Moraine

- the Kawartha Highlands
- Hastings County
- Lanark
- and even Algonquin's lower travel routes

If creatures migrate seasonally or maintain southern territories, they would absolutely use these corridors.

And the sightings confirm it.

July 13, 2013 — Off-Roaders Stuck in Mud Hear Knocking & Growling

When the forest responded to their engines

A family and friends off-roading north of Oshawa — the classic dirt-trail country of Raglan — got their truck stuck in deep mud at dusk.

That's when the forest changed.

From the treeline came:

- hard, deliberate knocks
- a deep growl
- slow movement circling the stuck vehicle

The family described the sound as "a warning… and a clear one."

What makes this case important:

1. It occurred in an area with heavy forest cover, surrounded by farm belts.

2. Whatever made the sounds approached *quietly*.

3. It stayed hidden but close.

4. It circled the group before retreating.

5. Growls were too deep for a cougar, and too sustained for a bear.

Knocking + growling = deliberate communication.

This wasn't random wildlife.
Something was saying:
"Leave."

Lanark County — Tracks in Snow, 2014

Clear impressions across an open field

A witness in Lanark County found a line of tracks crossing a snow-covered field.

The prints were:

- large
- human-like
- evenly spaced

- deep enough to indicate weight
- with no drag marks

They entered a cedar swamp and disappeared.

This wasn't far from the Raglan activity — and they share similar land characteristics: mixed hardwood forests, swamp belts, and ridges ideal for movement.

The fact that the creature crossed open field suggests confidence.

Most wildlife hugs tree lines.
This did not.

Lanark County — 2013 Sighting (189-13)

A figure moving at the edge of treeline

In 2013, just south of the snow crossing area, a witness reported a large figure moving upright along a treeline.

The creature was described as:

- tall
- uniform in colour
- moving deliberately
- not reacting to the witness
- disappearing behind brush without sound

This sighting pairs with the snowprints from the following year, indicating at least a two-year presence.

Durham-to-Lanark movement is plausible — and documented.

Puzzle Lake — July 28, 2013 — A Boulder Thrown Into the Water

A different kind of intimidation

Puzzle Lake Provincial Park is rugged, isolated, and far more wild than most southern Ontario parks. Kayakers often describe it as "northern" even though it's hours south of Temagami.

In 2013, a kayaker paddling near shore heard a thunderous splash.

A large boulder, not a rock, had been thrown into the lake.

This wasn't an avalanche.
Not a falling tree.
Not erosion.

The boulder entered the water at an angle consistent with a *throw*.

The witness saw movement on shore — a large dark form — before it slipped away.

Boulder-throwing is advanced behaviour.
It requires:

- massive strength
- intent

- accuracy

Puzzle Lake is prime territory for a creature with that kind of capability.

Kawartha Lakes — Ongoing Activity (142-13)

Prints found, family reports long-term encounters

A family living near Kawartha Lakes contacted investigators after repeated incidents:

- prints found on their property
- knocks heard at night
- something moving through the bush
- strange vocalizations near their cabin
- impressions near their shed
- tracks leading through marsh behind their home

Investigators stayed overnight with the family and photographed prints — wide, flat, deep, and spaced too far apart for human stride.

This is one of the strongest southern Ontario patterns:

Durham → Kawartha Lakes → Peterborough Highlands is a travel corridor.

And this family sits right on it.

South of Sunderland — Tracks in a Marsh (139-12)

Wetland prints preserved perfectly

In 2012, tracks were found in a marsh south of Sunderland.

The land there:

- is thick
- swampy
- remote despite being south-central
- full of old trapline and ATV routes

The prints were:

- clear
- deep
- well-formed
- showing toe definition

This marsh lies directly west of the Raglan trail system.

These creatures were not wandering randomly.
They were moving through a known corridor.

Raglan / Oshawa Region — July 2013 (148-13)

A family trapped in mud hears the forest come alive

This ties directly into the earlier Raglan account:

A family stuck in a mud bog off-road heard:

- sharp wood knocks
- low growls
- movement pacing the treeline
- brush shifting
- silence before each knock

These were not random noises.
They were patterned.

Witnesses described the growls as "too human to be a bear, too animal to be a human."

That line always stays with me.

Hastings County — 1988 Creature Pressing on Tent (147-88)

A childhood memory that never faded

In 1988 near Foxboro, a 10-year-old and several others were camping when something:

- pressed large hands onto the side of their tent
- shook the fabric
- made heavy footfalls around the camp
- then ran off into the woods with incredible speed

The hand impressions were wide — far wider than a human hand.

This account is chilling because:

1. Children rarely embellish; they recall fear, not details.
2. Multiple witnesses experienced the same event.
3. The creature pressed down on the tent gently — not violently.
4. Running speed suggested upright, powerful movement.

This is one of southern Ontario's earliest, clearest contact cases.

Halton County — March 30, 2013 Track in Mud (144-13)

A family hiking finds an enormous print

A man and his two children were hiking in a conservation area when they discovered a 15–16 inch track in thick mud.

Key details:

- toes clearly defined
- wide heel base
- deep pressure ridge
- no collapse in arch (suggesting flat primate-like foot)

What makes this important:

Halton County is not remote — but the print was found deep enough in the conservation area to be far from casual hikers.

The print's depth and width were consistent with:

- extreme weight
- bipedal motion
- anatomical accuracy

Southern Ontario has fewer physical track findings.
This is one of the best.

How Durham County Fits Into the Larger Picture

When I mapped all Durham-area sightings with the Kawartha, Hastings, Lanark, and Halton activity, a startling truth emerged:

Durham County is the southern anchor of a massive wilderness corridor extending all the way to Algonquin.

Points of alignment:

- Oshawa ↔ Sunderland ↔ Kawartha Lakes
- Kawartha Lakes ↔ Bancroft ↔ Hastings
- Hastings ↔ Lanark ↔ Calabogie
- Lanark ↔ Madawaska ↔ Algonquin Park

This corridor is:

- densely forested
- sparsely patrolled
- rich in wetland
- full of wildlife
- interconnected through river systems

A creature could move hundreds of kilometers without crossing a major highway.

And based on the sightings, it does.

Behavior in the Durham Region

The creature — or creatures — here tend to show:

1. Territorial Warnings

Knocks
Growls
Boulder throws

2. Marshland Movement

Sunderland
Lanark
Kawartha Lakes

3. Cabin Proximity

Kawartha family experiences

4. Hands-on Interaction

Foxboro tent incident

5. Roadside Boldness

Figures along treelines (Lanark and Hastings)

6. Established Consistency

Reports spanning decades

These aren't wanderers drifting south.
These are creatures using this region as part of a seasonal or permanent route.

What Durham County Has Taught Me

Durham County surprised me.

It taught me that the mystery isn't confined to the deep north — that it breathes just as strongly in the southern wild pockets:

- the cedar swamps
- the off-road trails
- the farmland edges
- the forgotten crown land
- the marsh belts
- and the quiet conservation forests

What I learned here:

1. Southern Ontario is not "too populated" — not in the places that matter.

2. These creatures are far more adaptable than most researchers believe.

3. They are comfortable operating close to human noise — as long as cover exists.

4. The Durham–Kawartha–Lanark corridor may be a key southern travel route.

5. Behaviour here is more confrontational than in Algonquin or Temagami.

**6. Something is using Durham the way a predator uses the edge of a field:

to observe, to move, to hunt, and to remain unseen.**

Durham County is the southern threshold of Ontario's Bigfoot mystery.
And once you understand the movement patterns here, the entire map of Ontario begins to make sense.

This region closes the loop.

CHAPTER 10 — EASTERN ONTARIO: THE QUIET WATCHERS OF THE MAPLE FRONTIER

Eastern Ontario is a study in contrasts.

It's a place where farmland rolls into deep cedar forests, where sleepy small towns sit only minutes from rugged wilderness, where the Canadian Shield begins to crack through the soil and reveal ancient stone beneath. It's a region shaped by rivers — the Ottawa, the Madawaska, the Rideau — and by the long, hard winters that drive everything into survival mode.

On the surface, Eastern Ontario looks tamer than much of the province.
It isn't.

Hidden behind the farmland and the lakeside cottages is a world of thick corridors, rock ridges, forgotten hunt camps, old snowmobile trails, and maple bush so dense it swallows sound. It's also an area where law enforcement officers, truck drivers, families, hunters, and completely ordinary people have seen things they cannot explain.

The reports here aren't dramatic.
They're *sharp*.
Precise.
And unsettling in a different way from the north.

Eastern Ontario is not a land of roaring vocalizations and rock-throwing.
It is a land of sudden appearances, silent crossings, and uncomfortable proximity.

The creatures here — whatever they are — seem to move with quiet intention.

And the encounters tend to happen up close.

Let's start with the one that still resurfaces every few years — the police officer's story.

October 2003 — The Toronto Police Officer Who Saw Too Much

Moose hunting near the Ottawa Valley — and a creature that shouldn't exist

You don't forget a report from a trained police officer.
They're taught to observe.
To identify threat.
To stay calm under stress.

This witness was off duty, hunting moose with a partner in a remote part of the Ottawa Valley. Early morning light, cool air, leaves wet from overnight rain. Perfect moose conditions.

They moved quietly along an overgrown logging road, scanning cuts and marsh edges.

Then something stepped out ahead of them.

Not a moose.
Not a bear.
Not a human.

The officer described:

- a tall, broad figure

- dark, uniform hair

- a head rising far higher than any man

- long arms that swung with primate-like motion

- a smell like "wet fur mixed with earth"

- absolute silence

- and an impossible stride as it crossed the clearing

It looked at them — not startled, not panicked — and continued into the treeline with the fluid movement of something that belonged there.

The officer froze.
His partner whispered, "What the hell was that?"

Neither of them had an answer.

They left the woods early.
The officer later contacted researchers not for attention, but because the sighting troubled him.
Deeply.

It still does.

December 2004 — The Trucker Who Watched a Giant Cross the Highway

A pre-dawn encounter west of Toronto

Around 5 a.m., a long-haul trucker was driving 40 miles west of Toronto along a rural section of highway when the unimaginable happened.

Something crossed the road in front of his truck.

A large, upright figure — too tall for a human, too heavy for a deer, too broad for a bear — moving quickly from one treeline to the next.

The trucker slammed the brakes.
The figure never turned.
Its stride was long, fluid, and powerful.

He described:

- a "man-shape but not a man"
- hair visible even in low light
- shoulders nearly as wide as the lane
- absolute silence as it moved
- a purposeful, confident crossing

Trucks don't scare wildlife easily.

But whatever this was didn't care about the truck at all.

It acted like something that had crossed that road many times before.

December 2006 — A Father and Son See Something in the Trees

North of Brockville — the creature that moved too easily

Driving home from an evening visit, a father and son traveled a quiet county road north of Brockville. The land there rolls between farmland and pockets of dense hardwood forest.

As they rounded a bend, their headlights caught movement.

A large figure stepped between trees — upright, dark, broad.

It moved:

- quickly
- smoothly
- without hesitation
- slipping between trees with impossible agility

The father slowed the car.
Both watched as the creature crossed the ditch and vanished into a pine stand.

The son remembers saying:
"Dad… that wasn't a deer."

The father whispered back:
"I know."

They told no one for years.

Markdale, 1995 — Strange Vocalizations in the Night

The sound that didn't match anything known

Markdale sits on the western edge of the Eastern Ontario influence — a region of mixed farmland, forest, and hills. In August 1995, residents reported a series of loud, strange vocalizations echoing through a forested valley.

Descriptions included:

- long, rising howls
- deep chest resonance
- a tone that didn't match coyote or dog
- a feeling that something large produced the sound

Locals compared it to a "cross between a man yelling and a wolf calling."

It was heard again the next night.

Then never again.

Vocalizations like this are extremely rare in Eastern Ontario. Most encounters here are visual.

That makes this case important.
It suggests that whatever moves through these lands is capable of classic Sasquatch vocal behaviour — even if it rarely uses it.

Patterns of Behaviour in Eastern Ontario

When all sightings from the region are examined together, several consistent traits emerge.

1. Silent, Fluid Movement

All three major roadside sightings involve creatures moving silently and smoothly across open areas.

2. Close Proximity

Encounters often happen at short distances — 30 to 60 meters.

3. Edge Habitat Preference

These creatures stay near:

- treelines
- marsh edges
- road cuts
- hydro corridors
- long, narrow forest belts

They use the terrain the same way deer and coyotes do — but move like something far larger.

4. Minimal Vocal Activity

Unlike Thunder Bay and Temagami, Eastern Ontario sees:

- no extended howls
- no whoops
- no aggressive calls

Instead, these creatures remain quiet — watchful, not confrontational.

5. Road Crossings

The number of roadside sightings is unusually high.

This suggests confidence.
Or familiarity.

Or both.

Why Eastern Ontario Works for a Large, Elusive Creature

Eastern Ontario is busier than the deep north — but it's also more fragmented, more overgrown, and more full of hidden pockets than people realize.

Key factors:

1. Complex Habitat

Hardwood forest, cedar swamp, granite ridges, river systems.

2. Low Night Activity

Most rural residents are indoors by dark.

3. Abundant Wildlife

Whitetail deer populations explode in this region.

4. Vast Private Land

Large tracts of forest that aren't publicly accessible.

5. River Corridors

Key routes that allow movement north and south with little human interference.

Creatures that avoid confrontation could easily thrive here.

The Eastern Ontario Signature

Every region in Ontario has its "signature" behaviour.

Temagami is long-term territory.
Sudbury is frequent contact.
Kenora is deep-range wilderness.
Thunder Bay is bold, loud dominance.

Eastern Ontario?

Eastern Ontario is presence.

Silent.
Close.

Hidden.
Watching.

The creatures here aren't trying to scare anyone, and they aren't trying to leave. They coexist quietly, skirting the edges of human activity, appearing only when movement brings them to roads, swamps, or forest margins.

Their behaviour suggests intelligence — not avoidance, not aggression, but choice.

They let themselves be seen only when they decide to.

What Eastern Ontario Has Taught Me

This region changed my perception of Bigfoot in southern and central Ontario.

It taught me that:

1. These creatures aren't just deep-wilderness specialists.

They can live in fragmented forest systems.

2. They move with precision and intention.

3. They thrive where people assume the land is too developed.

4. They use edge habitats better than any known mammal.

5. They are active at dawn and dusk more than at night.

6. They are closer to us than we think — often only one treeline away.

Eastern Ontario is a region where the mystery feels close to the surface.
Not ancient and distant like the north.
Not violent and storm-beaten like Superior.

Here, the mystery is quiet.
Alive.
Patient.

Watching from the shadows of maple stands and cedar thickets, walking the edges of county roads at dawn, slipping between barn shadows and forest corridors with a confidence that does not belong to any known animal.

Eastern Ontario is proof:
Ontario's Bigfoot mystery is province-wide — not confined to remote wilderness.

And sometimes the closest encounters happen not in the deep woods, but in the places where forests touch the edge of the everyday world.

CHAPTER 11 — PARRY SOUND DISTRICT: THE SHADOWS OF GEORGIAN BAY

Parry Sound District is the kind of place that fools you if you don't know it well.

To anyone driving Highway 400, it looks like cottage country — a patchwork of lakes, pines bending in the wind, and pink granite rising out of the earth like exposed bone. But once you leave the highway, once you leave the rental cottages and the marinas and the familiar pockets of summer traffic, you realize something:

Parry Sound is not southern Ontario.
Not really.
Not once you get off the main roads.

It's a maze of inland lakes, forgotten logging corridors, islands that stretch to the horizon, and deep corridors of spruce and cedar where no trail has existed for decades. It's a place where cellphone reception dies, where night falls fast, where sound behaves strangely, and where you begin to understand why people have been seeing things here for nearly half a century.

And if there's one region in all of Ontario where Bigfoot sightings show a kind of quiet persistence — not dramatic, not loud, not constant, but steady — it's here.

Parry Sound is the quiet heartbeat between the heavily populated south and the vast northern wilderness.
And that makes it special.

For me, this region holds something else too — something personal.

Years ago, long before I began pulling together the massive archives and case files that now form the backbone of this book, I made my own trip into this country. I paddled across a cold, wind-chopped lake and camped on the very island where, years later, two hunters would hear one of the clearest vocalizations ever reported in southern Ontario.

I didn't know it then.
I was simply following up on a rumor — a 2010 vocalization report that had barely circulated among a few researchers. But I went. I camped there. And the memory of that night stayed with me in a way I didn't expect.

Nothing major happened.
No creature walked through my camp.
No howl shattered the dark.
No prints were found.

But the silence was wrong.
The island felt watched.
The air felt charged.

And when the 2024 vocalization occurred there — fourteen years after I sat under the same canopy of pines — I understood something about this region that I hadn't fully grasped before:

Parry Sound is long-term territory.
Something lives here.
Something that doesn't leave.

And it has been here much longer than any of us realized.

Let's begin where the record begins — at the window.

1978 — The ORF Pilot Plant Window Incident (Case 193-78)

Two workers see something staring back at them

Tiny Township, Parry Sound District — winter, 1978.

Two night-shift workers at the ORF Pilot Plant were going through the kind of mundane tasks that only happen in remote industrial buildings. A windless night. Light snow drifting down. A stillness that always seems heavier in the bush.

And then one of them noticed a shadow at the window.

At first he thought it was his reflection — a trick of light. But as he looked closer, the "reflection" didn't move when he did. It moved on its own. It leaned forward. It filled the upper half of the window. A face emerged from the dark behind the glass.

Not human.
Not animal in the way we understand animals.

A towering figure, covered in dark hair, stood inches from the window, eyes level with the men inside. The workers described:

- a broad, flat face
- deep-set, intelligent eyes
- dark hair around the jaw and forehead
- shoulders so wide they stretched beyond the frame
- breath fogging the glass ever so slightly

And then, as if realizing it had been seen, the creature stepped back, turned, and vanished into the night without a sound.

No bear stands upright at full height and presses its face to a window without leaving claw marks. No person wanders deep into the winter bush at night to scare two workers and then walks away silently through snow.

This is one of Ontario's earliest high-credibility encounters. And it matters because it establishes something crucial:

Parry Sound activity isn't new.
It has roots.
Deep roots.

Bear Lake, 2014 — The Voice That Shook the Trees (Case 187-15)

The howl that didn't belong to any known animal

Bear Lake lies north of Parry Sound, where the roads thin and the forest grows heavy around the water. In 2014, a witness sitting outside near dusk heard a sound roll across the lake — a howl so deep it seemed to vibrate through the air rather than travel through it.

They described:

- a chest-deep resonance
- a rise in pitch like a siren winding itself upward
- a long, sustained breath

- power behind the sound, enough to carry across the entire lake

- a sudden, unnatural silence afterward

Wolves don't howl alone with that kind of force.
Coyotes yip, bark, and chorus.
Moose call in nasal, wavering tones.

This was different.
It was structured.
Resonant.
Huge.

The witness said:

"It felt like something was announcing itself. Not to another animal, but to the entire forest."

Bear Lake sits along a natural wildlife corridor that connects Magnetawan, Parry Sound, and the Georgian Bay interior. If a creature were maintaining territory here, this is exactly where it would broadcast.

But if Bear Lake offered the voice, Naiscoot Lake offered the mystery.

Pre-2010 — The Naiscoot Lake Rail Bed Encounter

The creature that did not yield the path

Before 2010, a man walking a long-abandoned railway line near the western end of Naiscoot Lake experienced something unusual — something that still circulates in hushed tones among researchers.

As he walked, he saw a figure on the tracks ahead of him.
Not crossing the tracks.
Walking toward him.

Details reported:

- upright

- tall — well over 7 feet

- dark, uniform hair

- long arms swinging deliberately

- a forward-hunched but powerful posture

- no sign of hesitation

- no sign of fear

The creature continued down the rail bed directly toward him with slow, steady, confident strides. Finally, the man stepped off the tracks and let it pass. He never heard it move into the brush. It simply vanished.

This behaviour — advancing instead of withdrawing — is rare in Ontario reports. Most creatures avoid direct confrontation. But this one held its ground.

It suggested territory.
Ownership.
A long-term presence at Naiscoot.

And this is what brought me to the lake years later — though I didn't know the full weight of the history when I went.

2010 — My Island Investigation on Naiscoot Lake

The silence that said more than sound ever could

It was early fall when I paddled across Naiscoot Lake, heading toward a small island east of the later 2024 vocalization site. I had heard only fragments of a story — a possible howl years earlier, told second-hand, nothing solid. But something about the area had come up in enough reports that I felt compelled to see it for myself.

The lake was cold, the water black under cloud cover. Pines leaned over the shoreline like they were studying the surface. There was no breeze that day — no loon calls, no distant engines, nothing but the sound of my paddle slipping through water.

I reached the island in late afternoon, set up a small camp, and walked the perimeter. The island wasn't large — a cluster of pines, a sweep of granite, old lichen, a place untouched except for the occasional canoeist landing for lunch.

I stayed the night.

Nothing dramatic happened.
No howls split the dark.
No heavy footsteps approached camp.
No knocks echoed across the lake.

But the silence was wrong.

It was dense, heavy, the kind of silence that makes you turn your head every few minutes even when you know you shouldn't. The air felt thick. The island felt occupied even though I was alone. Several times, as I sat by the dying coals of my fire, I felt the distinct sensation that something was watching from the treeline.

I remember writing in my field notes:

"This place feels held. Like something has claim to it."

I left in the morning. But the memory of that night — the stillness, the weight of the air, the sense of presence — stayed with me.

Fourteen years later, two hunters would hear exactly what I had been waiting for.

And suddenly everything about that 2010 trip made sense.

October 21, 2024 — Naiscoot Lake Island: The Night the Forest Answered

Two hunters hear the call I never heard — but always expected

Two hunters camped on the very island east of my old campsite heard something break the silence at 9:30 p.m.

Not a moose.
Not a wolf.
Not an echo of human activity.

A howl — long, deep, resonant, and layered with a tone no known animal in Ontario can match.

It began low, rose into a sustained bellow, fractured into a throat-deep growl, then ended abruptly.

The hunters described:

- tremendous volume
- chest reverberation
- multiple tonal changes
- a sense of direction but not distance
- instant silence afterward

The forest switched off.
Everything stopped.

One hunter whispered,
"That was close."

The other answered,
"No. That was big."

This vocalization matched the structure of Sasquatch howls documented in North America:

- deep initial breath
- head-tilted resonance
- long lung capacity
- controlled pitch modulation

The hunters left the island at first light.

When I heard their report, the memory of my 2010 night sharpened into focus.
The silence I had felt wasn't emptiness.
It was waiting.

Understanding the Parry Sound Landscape

This region offers perfect habitat for an intelligent, reclusive species:

1. The Islands

Georgian Bay's labyrinth of islands offers isolation, denning areas, and escape routes no predator or human can easily follow.

2. Granite Ridges

High ground with visibility — perfect for movement and observation.

3. Deep Interior Lakes

Cold, remote waters where few people camp outside peak summer.

4. Large Continuous Forest

Fewer roads.
Fewer houses.
Plenty of cover.

5. Water Corridors

Lakes and shallow channels act as quiet highways.

A creature could live here for decades with minimal human interference.

And the sightings reflect exactly that.

The Parry Sound Behavioural Pattern

Across all cases, certain behaviours remain consistent:

1. Close-range curiosity

The ORF window case shows direct observation — unusual but telling.

2. Vocal territory marking

Bear Lake and Naiscoot Island both produced high-volume calls.

3. Silent dominance

The 2010 rail encounter and my own 2010 island experience share this quality:
A presence that reveals itself not through noise, but through *silence*.

4. Long-term return patterns

The 1978, 2010, 2014, and 2024 events form a timeline of activity spanning nearly half a century.

5. Geographic consistency

All incidents fall within the same corridor of lakes and islands.

This is not random.
This is not scattered.
This is not occasional.

This is a region being used — regularly.

The Parry Sound Hypothesis: A Permanent Southern Population

Based on all the evidence, Parry Sound District likely hosts:

- a resident breeding population

- using islands as refuges

- maintaining a territory boundary extending from Bear Lake through Naiscoot into the inland channels

- with individuals who have learned to observe from close range

- and who rarely, if ever, leave the region

It may be the strongest southern cousin to the deep-north populations of Temagami and Sudbury.

And it may be older than any of us realize.

What Parry Sound Has Taught Me

This region taught me things I didn't expect — not about the creatures themselves, but about persistence, territory, and what it means for a creature to share land with people who rarely realize it.

1. These creatures observe us up close.

The ORF window incident is undeniable.

2. They do not abandon good territory.

1978 → 2010 → 2014 → 2024
Same region.
Same behaviour.
Same presence.

3. Silence can be as meaningful as sound.

My 2010 night proved that.

4. Vocalizations mark territory deliberately.

Naiscoot and Bear Lake show structured calling.

5. Islands hold more secrets than mainland forest.

Creatures use water barriers strategically.

6. The mystery isn't far away — it's just unseen.

Parry Sound proves Bigfoot doesn't require vast, untouched wilderness.

It requires structure, cover, food, and corridors.

Parry Sound gives all four.

And somewhere on those islands, among the twisted pines and black water, something old still walks — quiet, aware, and far more intelligent than the wilderness myths suggest.

It watched two workers through a window in 1978.
It walked a rail bed in 2010.
It howled across the lake in 2014.
It roared in 2024.

And long before any of us heard it —
long before anybody put a name to it —
it was already here.

CHAPTER 12 — SOUTHWEST COUNTIES: THE FOG COUNTRY SHADOWS

Southwestern Ontario is not the place most people think of when they talk about Bigfoot.

When you picture Sasquatch, you picture the north — vast forests, deep lakes, fog rolling off bogs, and wilderness so wide you can disappear in it. You don't picture the rolling farmland between London and Woodstock, the dune beaches near Grand Bend, the tall cornfields of Huron County, or the patchwork of forest strips that thread between tobacco country, dairy farms, and old river valleys.

But that's the mistake most people make.

Southwestern Ontario is *not* too developed.
It's *not* too flat.
It's *not* too populated.

It's fragmented wilderness — forest belts, cedar swamps, river corridors, conservation areas, and old farm woodlots stitched together like a hidden network. A creature with intelligence and the ability to move silently through tight cover could live here for decades without anyone ever getting a clear look.

And yet people *have* gotten looks.
More than they realize.

They've heard things too — things that aren't coyotes, aren't foxes, and definitely aren't something you want to hear while camping in a thin belt of trees beside a warm southwestern night.

This region might not feel like Kenora, or Sudbury, or Temagami —
but it holds its own kind of darkness.

A subtle one.
A quiet one.
A *close* one.

And the encounters here carry something that stands out: boldness near human space, with sightings happening at farms, treatment plants, riverbeds, and town edges.

Let's start near the dunes of Lake Huron, where the forest screamed.

2015 — Grand Bend: Screams in the Dark (Case 191-15)

When the night turned on itself

Grand Bend is summer country — sand dunes, warm water, cottages, fireworks, and campfires. But go ten minutes inland and the landscape changes. Forest thickens. Marshes appear. The land sinks into cedar swamps that barely dry in August.

In 2015, a couple camping outside Grand Bend heard something scream from deep inside a nearby woodlot.

Not a coyote.
Not a fox.
Not an owl, fisher, or bobcat.

A human-like scream — long, high, and loaded with power.

The witnesses described:

- a rise in pitch that felt unnatural

- a sustained volume that didn't match any known animal

- a "forced, almost furious" tone

- silence afterward — immediate, oppressive, complete

They stayed awake the entire night, listening.

No second scream came.
No movement.
No howls.
Just the feeling that the scream had been a warning — not for them, but for something else in the woods.

Grand Bend is a node — a connection point between the Huron shoreline and the deep interior forests stretching toward Exeter and the Huron–Perth backcountry.

This scream wasn't random.
It was placed.

And it wasn't the only sign.

2015 — Woodstock: The Footprint in the Mud (Case 188-15)

A single print that defied dismissal

Near Woodstock, a landowner walking a muddy creek edge found a single deep print —
15 inches long, wide, flat, with clear toe definition.

There were no other prints nearby.

That's the detail skeptics jump on — but experienced trackers know better:

- solitary prints happen when something steps from rock to mud

- or from log to mud

- or from bank to mud

- or from marsh grass to solid ground

The print was:

- deep — indicating weight

- clean — indicating deliberate, controlled step

- without drag — meaning bipedal

- far too wide for a human

- anatomically correct in toe layout

The landowner knew wildlife tracks well.
This wasn't bear.
Not even remotely.

The footprint faced toward a stretch of forest that connects to Whiteman's Creek and eventually into Brant County.

That connection matters.

Because only months earlier, something walked across a road near the Six Nations Reserve.

February 2013 — The Water Treatment Plant Workers (Case 153-13)

Three men see a creature that should not exist — and all three agree

Few modern sightings have three witnesses.
Even fewer have three sober, working men on shift.

At a Water Treatment Plant near the Six Nations Reserve, three workers saw a creature cross the road in front of them.

They described:

- a tall, black figure
- upright
- wide-shouldered
- with arms longer than a man's
- a stride too big to be human
- and movement that looked effortless

It didn't look at them.
It didn't run.
It walked across the road and vanished into the brush like it had done it a thousand times.

The men talked about it later — quietly, cautiously — and realized they all saw the same thing. Exactly the same thing.

Tracks were found days later near Whiteman's Creek.

You'll notice that water appears often in southwestern cases — creeks, rivers, irrigation routes, swamps.
Water is a perfect silent travel corridor.

But the strangest Brant County case didn't involve workers.

It involved an old woman in a small town who came face-to-face with something she never expected.

Saint George / Brantford — The Terrified Witness (Case 154-13)

The creature she never forgot

Near Saint George, north of Brantford, an older woman living alone witnessed something outside her home — something she struggled to even describe afterward.

Late at night, she saw a figure near the treeline behind her property. She assumed it was a trespasser.
Then it stepped into the open.

She described:

- shoulders wider than her doorway

- a height she estimated as "almost touching the soffit"

- dark, heavy hair

- long arms that hung low

- a head shaped more like a gorilla's than a man's

- no sound as it moved

- and eyes that reflected a dull, deep orange

She froze.
The creature froze.
And then it moved away into the forest at a speed she later called "unnatural."

This case matters for one reason:
She had no interest in Bigfoot, no exposure to the subject, no reason to embellish.

And she never once described it as "a man."

Not once.

Whiteman's Creek — A Hidden Corridor

Whiteman's Creek is one of the most important natural corridors in southern Ontario:

- thick forest belts

- long marsh sections

- minimal development

- limited access points

- deer-rich habitat
- deep gully systems
- sound-absorbing cedar stands

If a creature needed to travel between:

- Huron County
- Brant County
- Six Nations
- Woodstock
- Grand Bend
- or the Norfolk woodlots,

this is exactly the river system it would use.

And the sightings suggest exactly that.

The Geography of the Southwest Mystery

Southwestern Ontario is not "flat farmland."
It's a puzzle of:

- gorge networks
- deep ravines
- reclaimed forests

- massive conservation blocks
- swamp belts running east–west
- abandoned rail lines
- drainage corridors
- hidden pine plantations
- river systems loaded with cover

A creature that avoids confrontation could travel for hundreds of kilometers without crossing a major road.

Most people never see the interior of Huron County.
Most people never walk the back ravines of Norfolk.
Most people never go into the swamp-laced corridors west of Woodstock.

Those who do often come back saying the same thing:

"It's a lot wilder than I expected."

And the sightings prove them right.

Huron County, 1987 — The Cornfield Crossing (Case 166-87)

The creature that stepped out of the corn

In 1987, south of Exeter, a witness driving at dusk saw a massive shape emerge from a cornfield, walk across the road, and disappear into the opposite field.

Details:

- upright
- uniform dark hair
- easily seven feet tall
- long arms
- smooth, confident stride
- no signs of stumbling on the uneven ground

Cornfields are perfect cover.
Animals use them constantly — deer, coyotes, even cougars.

But nothing walks upright through a cornfield that tall with that kind of ease.

The witness said:

"It didn't move like it was pushing through stalks. It moved like the corn parted for it."

That phrasing is important.
Two other southwest witnesses — years apart — said the same thing.

Behaviour Patterns in the Southwest Counties

When all reports from Huron, Brant, Woodstock, Grand Bend, Norfolk, and the adjacent counties are combined, a unique behavioural profile emerges:

1. Road Crossings

This region has more road-crossing sightings than almost anywhere else in Ontario.

2. Edge Habitat Use

These creatures use:

- cornfield edges
- creek edges
- river edges
- woodlot edges
- gully rims

3. Large Territory Range

Reports cluster along north–south and east–west movement lines.

4. Night Vocalizations

The Grand Bend scream is rare but consistent with other southern-type reports.

5. Curiosity Near Structures

The Saint George case is one of the closest southern encounters.

6. Water-Based Movement

Creeks and tributaries offer silent navigation.

7. Solitary Individuals

Unlike the north, most southwestern sightings involve single creatures — not family groups.

This suggests a different style of habitat use:
low-density population, wide movement range.

Why the Southwest Makes Sense for Bigfoot

Most people assume Bigfoot can only survive in deep northern bush.
But the evidence in southwestern Ontario contradicts that.

Here's why the southwest works:

1. High Deer Population

The densest whitetail populations in Canada are in southern Ontario.

2. Abundant Water

Creeks, rivers, marsh systems, and ponds.

3. Thick Undergrowth

Brush, cedar, cattails, and dogwood — all ideal for concealment.

4. Night Quiet

Few people explore after dark.

5. Fragmented but Connected Forest

Perfect for an animal that prefers edges.

6. Agriculture Waste

Grain, corn, soy — food sources for deer, and passively for predators that follow them.

7. Old Forest Pockets

Large conservation blocks in Norfolk, Huron, Perth, and Brant provide core shelter zones.

This region supports black bear, cougar, lynx, coyotes, wolves (intermittently), and enormous deer herds.

A primate?
Not unbelievable — not in practice, not in ecology.

What the Southwest Has Taught Me

Southwestern Ontario sits at the opposite end of the map from Kenora, Thunder Bay, and Temagami, but it taught me lessons that echo through every chapter of this book.

1. Bigfoot doesn't require uninterrupted wilderness.

It needs corridors — and the southwest has thousands of them.

2. These creatures adapt better than we think.

They use farmland edges the same way deer do.

3. Movement here is deliberate and silent.

The creatures don't vocalize often — but when they do, it's unmistakable.

4. They may use the southwest as winter territory.

Less snow, easier food access, mild climate.

5. They stay close to water systems.

Whiteman's Creek, the Ausable River, the Maitland, the Grand.

6. People see them more than they admit.

Truckers.
Farmers.
Late-night commuters.
Shift workers.

Witnesses come from all walks of life — and the patterns match those of legitimate sightings across North America.

Southwestern Ontario proves something essential:

Bigfoot isn't just a creature of the deep north.
It's a creature of opportunity, intelligence, and adaptation.

And here, in the fragmented wilderness between farms and forest patches, it walks routes that have existed long before any of the roads that now cross them.

CHAPTER 13 — SIMCOE COUNTY: THE GATEWAY BETWEEN WORLDS

Simcoe County sits in a strange transition zone — a place where southern Ontario begins to fall away and the northern wild begins to rise. It's a land of hardwood bush, rolling moraine ridges, long river valleys, cedar swamps, and quiet farm roads that stretch into dark pockets nobody visits after sunset.

Simcoe is both busy and empty.
Crowded and forgotten.
Tamed and absolutely untamed in the places that matter.

People don't think of Simcoe County as "Bigfoot Country."
But anyone who spends real time in those forests — the ones behind New Lowell, Minesing, Angus, Anten Mills, New Tecumseh, and Oro-Medonte — knows the truth:

Simcoe County has a lot more wilderness than most people realize.

Large tracts of it.

And in those tracts, people have been hearing and seeing things for decades.

Not dramatic, attention-grabbing encounters.
Not the roaring, howling, territorial shows of Thunder Bay.
Not the close-range dominance of Naiscoot Lake.
And not the roadside giants of Cochrane.

Simcoe's mystery is quieter.
More contained.
A presence that stays just out of view — but never out of mind.

Because Simcoe County is a crossroads.
A meeting ground between southern populations and northern ones.
A place where movement patterns converge into corridors of shadow.

And one of those corridors runs right through New Tecumseh.

November 12, 2013 — New Tecumseh: The Midnight Voices (Case 156-13)

The sounds that didn't belong to any animal in southern Ontario

It was just after midnight when the witness stepped outside behind their rural property in New Tecumseh. The air was cold, still, and soaked with the kind of silence that feels heavy on the skin.

Then it came.

A long, rising vocalization, far deeper than a coyote, far longer than a fox call, far too resonant to be anything small.

It wasn't a moose.
It wasn't a dog.
And it wasn't a human yelling from a distance.

It came again — a second call, lower this time, almost mournful, echoing through the swale of mixed hardwood and cedar behind the property.

Then a third — shorter, sharper, as if answering something only it could hear.

Each call carried:

- a resonance deeper than wolf
- a human-like articulation
- chest volume
- long breath capacity
- a sense of *intention*

The witness described the effect as:

"It felt like something big was announcing itself, but not to me. Like it was calling to something else in the woods."

What rattled them wasn't the vocalization itself.
It was the silence afterward.

Coyotes usually respond in packs.
Dogs bark.
Foxes chatter.

Here, everything went dead quiet.

New Tecumseh sits at a convergence point:

- Cedar swamp belts
- Hardwood hills
- Creek systems leading toward Nottawasaga River

- Corridors linking east toward Kawartha Lakes and west toward Grey County

This is excellent habitat for a creature that needs cover, water, and mobility.

And the midnight calls fit a pattern repeated in other parts of Simcoe:
rare vocalizations that appear once, then never again.

This is not random noise.
This is presence.

Quiet presence.

Simcoe County's Hidden Wilderness

The average person sees Simcoe County as cottages, beaches, farms, and ski hills.

But that's not the real Simcoe.

The real Simcoe is:

- the Minesing Wetlands — a vast, swampy expanse larger and more remote than most people imagine

- the endless forest belts between Angus and Base Borden

- the river valleys that snake through thick cover

- the moraine ridges of Oro-Medonte

- the deep interior forests near Washago

- the hinterlands that bleed into Muskoka
- the unbroken stretches connecting to Georgian Bay and the French River route

This land supports:

- moose
- black bear
- huge deer populations
- wolves in certain pockets
- and a converging ecosystem that mixes north and south wildlife

Simcoe County is not a suburban spillover.

It's a wild corridor masked by civilization.

And creatures that thrive in edge habitat — forests pressed against farms, wetlands pressed against ridges — would find no better place to live unnoticed.

Forests That Hide What Shouldn't Be There

Simcoe's forest structure supports stealth:

1. Dense Understory

Cedar, dogwood, and buckthorn offer heavy visual cover year-round.

2. Swamp Systems

Creatures can move silently through cattail and muskeg belts.

3. Old Logging Roads

Overgrown trails create perfect biped travel corridors.

4. Sound-Dampening Terrain

Wet forests swallow sound — perfect for an animal that avoids detection.

5. High Deer Density

Food is abundant.
Winterkill is frequent.
Predator presence is naturally supported.

This environment encourages movement — and that movement leaves traces.

Sightings Along the Corridors

Simcoe County sightings are spread thin on the surface — but line them up geographically and a clear structure emerges.

Almost all reports occur along:

- The Nottawasaga River system
- The Minesing Swamp perimeter

- Cedar belts near New Tecumseh
- The ridge lines north of Alliston
- The forest blocks stretching toward Highway 11
- The edges of conservation areas
- Transition zones between farm and forest

These corridors link directly to:

- Parry Sound District (northwest)
- Kawartha Lakes (east)
- Durham County (southeast)
- Grey County (west)
- Muskoka and Algonquin (directly north)

If a creature travels seasonally or migrates between territories — this is the exact intersection it would use.

Simcoe is not a hotspot by accident.
It is a crossroads of the province's wilderness flow.

Encounters That Don't Stay Still

Most Simcoe sightings follow patterns:

1. Short-lived vocalizations

One night.
One event.
Never repeated.

2. Edge-of-property movement

Something large walking along treelines, not entering yards.

3. Heavy footfalls

Witnesses report weight and biped cadence.

4. Occasional prints in mud

Large impressions near creeks and riverbeds.

5. Roadside glimpses

Dark figures slipping between stands of hardwood at dusk.

6. Animal reactions

Dogs whining, freezing, refusing to go near certain tracks.

7. Silence after the event

The woods go still — instantly.
Exactly like the deep north sightings.

These are not animals wandering from habitat.
These are animals moving with purpose.

Simcoe and the Minesing Wetlands Connection

The Minesing Wetlands are a key piece of the puzzle.

This sprawling marsh/swamp ecosystem is:

- enormous
- nearly impenetrable
- under-traveled
- full of natural blind spots
- rich with wildlife
- surrounded by forest
- notoriously difficult to search

If a creature needed a southern refuge, Minesing is almost perfect:

- few access points
- long stretches where humans never go
- thick vegetation
- deep natural channels
- vantage points along the perimeter
- abundant water

Many researchers have considered the Minesing region a likely "resting habitat" for transient or resident Bigfoot populations.

Simcoe County's sightings fit this theory perfectly.

Why Simcoe's Mystery Feels Different

Every region reveals a different personality:

- Temagami is ancient, territorial, and ongoing.
- Sudbury is busy, loud, and contact-heavy.
- Kenora is deep-range wilderness.
- Thunder Bay is bold and confrontational.
- Parry Sound is quiet dominance.
- Southwest Counties are stealth corridors.

Simcoe?
Simcoe is passing intelligence.

You can feel it in the reports:

- creatures that reveal themselves briefly
- vocalizations that come once
- movement along corridors instead of into properties
- sightings along ridge lines, not deep within forest
- a presence that feels temporary but aware

These creatures aren't based here permanently.
They move through.
They navigate with purpose.
They appear, disappear, reappear years later somewhere else along the same ecological highway.

Simcoe County is the intersection — the place where territorial lines blur and the wilderness of Ontario breathes in both directions.

What Simcoe County Has Taught Me

Simcoe taught me something important — something that changed how I view southern and central Ontario's Bigfoot presence.

1. Movement is as important as territory.

These creatures *travel*.
Simcoe is proof they move between regions.

2. Edge habitat is more valuable than deep forest.

Simcoe is a masterclass in edge-based living.

3. Short encounters can be more meaningful than dramatic ones.

One night of vocalizations can reveal a migration pattern.

4. The province's Bigfoot population is interconnected.

Simcoe lies between multiple hotspots.
It is the spoke in the wheel.

5. Silence can reveal intention.

After the New Tecumseh calls — silence.
This is classic territorial assertion.

6. There is no "too populated" region in Ontario for these creatures.

Only regions with enough cover and enough food.

Simcoe is proof that the mystery doesn't belong exclusively to the deep north.
It lives in the quiet corridors between places people assume are too settled, too farmland, too suburban.

The truth is this:

Ontario's wilderness is larger than people think — and Simcoe County is one of the provinces' secret passageways.

CHAPTER 14 — MUSKOKA: THE QUIET FOREST BETWEEN TWO WORLDS

Muskoka might be the most misunderstood region in Ontario.

When most people hear the name, they picture luxury cottages, blue water, boat wakes, and docks lined with Muskoka chairs. They picture summer heat rising off black rocks, the hum of outboard motors, the smell of sunscreen and cedar decks. They picture money — a lot of it — and the kind of curated wilderness that's been trimmed, polished, and made Instagram-safe.

But that Muskoka is only a thin strip along the lakes.

Step off the cottage roads, leave the marinas, follow one old bush road a few kilometers past where the pavement ends, and the façade falls away. The lakes shrink. The forest grows thicker. The ridges sharpen. The land reveals what it really is:

Wilderness. Real wilderness.
Not as remote as Temagami, not as brutal as Algonquin, not as rugged as Parry Sound, but a place where the land closes around you fast, and human presence is a thin layer on top of something far older.

And in that older layer — the one most people never see — something moves.

Something big.
Something quiet.
Something that uses Muskoka as a *corridor*, a *hunting range*, and a *buffer* between larger territories.

Muskoka is the meeting point between northern and southern Ontario.
It is the land between worlds.

And it has stories — more than most expect.

The Land That Hides More Than It Shows

To understand why Muskoka matters, you have to understand the terrain beneath the tourism.

Behind the resorts, highways, and rental cabins lies:

- Massive tracts of crown land
- Old logging corridors stretching 20–40 km into bush
- Storm-damaged pine forests with deep windfall cover
- Swamp systems rarely visited by humans
- Huge granite ridges offering vantage points
- Small, isolated lakes only accessible by canoe
- Quiet interior river systems linking to Algonquin
- Multi-thousand-acre private tracts with no public trails
- Seasonal areas empty nine months of the year

This isn't cottage country.
This is a place where black bear densities are high, wolves move

silently through cedar bottoms, and moose leave tracks bigger than a man's hand.

And it's exactly the kind of environment where a large, reclusive primate could move unseen.

Which brings us to the first pattern:
Muskoka is not a hotspot — it's a highway.

The Corridor Between Parry Sound and Algonquin

Every chapter before this one has built a picture:

- Parry Sound hosts long-term territory.

- Simcoe County is a southern crossroads.

- Algonquin is ancient, active, and vast.

- Sudbury connects westward.

- Temagami dominates the north.

But there is only one natural bridge between these regions: Muskoka.

Look at a map of forest cover, waterways, and crown land access:

- The forest from Parry Sound flows directly into western Muskoka.

- The interior of Muskoka rises into ridge systems that spill north toward Kearney, Magnetawan, and Burk's Falls.

- These ridges connect seamlessly into Algonquin's west gate and the Highway 60 interior region.

- On the eastern side, Muskoka's heavy forest press into Haliburton — another corridor that leads toward Kawartha Lakes and Durham.

If a creature needs to move between northern and southern ranges, Muskoka is the only region where:

- cover is continuous
- human density drops sharply once off pavement
- waterways offer quiet travel
- ridge lines prevent easy tracking
- there is food in all seasons

This is why Muskoka sightings often feel like "passing encounters."
They are glimpses — brief, unsettling, happening in places where nobody expects it.

And that's exactly what makes them credible.

The Sightings People Forget

Official reports from Muskoka are fewer in number than northern hotspots, but the *quality* of the accounts — the details, the witnesses, the locations — are notable.

Most common reports include:

1. Distant Biped Movement Seen at Dusk

Cottages on remote bays sometimes report a large, upright figure crossing a beaver meadow or ridge — too big and smooth to be a human, too upright to be a bear.

2. Heavy Footfalls Behind Campsites

Interior canoeists often describe nighttime pacing around distant camps, far louder than deer, slower than moose, and without the clumsiness of bears.

3. Wood Knocks

A surprisingly common element — sharp, single knocks heard on quiet lakes at dusk or dawn, sometimes answered from the opposite shore.

4. Long Howls in Off-Season

Multiple winter vocalizations reported near the borders of Algonquin Park — an extension of Algonquin's known patterns.

5. Tracks in Mud or Snow

Several hunters have reported long, flat, human-like impressions — often single tracks leading from rock to mud, a typical sign in rocky Shield terrain.

These sightings rarely make headlines.
They slip under the radar.
Muskoka locals talk quietly, if they talk at all.

But the accounts are consistent with known Bigfoot behaviour:

- short visibility
- silent retreat
- edge-of-territory movement
- seasonal passing

Which brings us to a phenomenon many researchers overlook:

Muskoka is where the creatures move — not where they stay.

The Muskoka–Algonquin Line: A Natural Choke Point

You can feel the difference in the air as you leave Huntsville and enter the western gates of Algonquin.

The forest grows taller.
The swamps grow deeper.
The nights grow quieter.
The wind shifts into something colder, older.

This line — this invisible ecological threshold — is where Muskoka transitions from mixed cottage wilderness to deep boreal gateway.

And almost all Muskoka sightings cluster near this threshold:

- Kearney
- Sprucedale
- Ravenscliffe

- Dwight
- Dorset
- Oxtongue Lake

These areas feed directly into Algonquin's western interior, which has recorded more sightings than any other region in Ontario except Temagami and Sudbury.

Creatures moving between territories wouldn't linger.
They would travel fast, quiet, direct.

But even movement leaves signs.

Late-Season Moose Hunts — The Unseen Watchers

Hunters in southern Muskoka have reported a strange phenomenon:

They feel watched.
Not by wolves.
Not by bears.
By something else.

Details include:

- heavy biped pacing at dusk
- deep branch breaks
- silence after movement

- occasional thrown stones

- vocalizations too deep for coyotes

- moose suddenly evacuating an area

Hunters know predatory behaviour.
They know when wolves are near.
They know when bears come through.
They know when the forest is normal.

What they describe in Muskoka is not normal.

It's something intelligent.
Something aware of them.
Something that follows parallel to their movement without revealing itself.

Classic territorial monitoring.

And these behaviours line up perfectly with documented patterns in Algonquin, Sudbury, and Temagami.

Midnight on the Logging Roads — The Shadow That Crosses

One of Muskoka's most consistent sighting types:

road-crossings at night.

These happen:

- on logging corridors

- on private forestry roads
- on backroads near Dwight and Dorset
- in areas where moose are common
- in shoulder seasons when cottages are empty

Witnesses describe:

- a tall, dark silhouette
- long stride
- arms swinging low
- crossing the road in 2–3 steps
- disappearing into dense forest without sound

These are near-identical to North Bay, Sudbury, and Cochrane reports.

And, importantly, these roads are rarely used at night — which means the creatures are comfortable navigating in low-risk areas, consistent with their behaviour across the province.

The Muskoka Silence Phenomenon

Many credible Muskoka witnesses — including canoeists, hunters, and long-time locals — describe something unique:

Sudden total silence in the forest.

No crickets.
No wind.
No owls.
No frogs.
No rustling.

Just absolute stillness.

This phenomenon is rare in southern regions but common in:

- Algonquin
- Temagami
- Thunder Bay
- Sudbury

Silence is a territorial marker — or a reaction to a predator.

In Muskoka, silence often appears *right before* a wood knock, distant step, or brief sighting.

And it appears consistently in the same wilderness blocks.

This is what convinced me that Muskoka is not random — it's patterned.

Muskoka as the Southern Edge of the Northern Population

This is the key insight:

Muskoka is not an isolated hotspot — it is the southern boundary of the northern population and the northern boundary of the southern migratory range.

It is where:

- Temagami creatures move south
- Algonquin creatures move west
- Parry Sound creatures move east
- Simcoe creatures move north
- Durham/Kawartha patterns intersect

It is a funnel.
A bridge.
A gateway.

This makes Muskoka critical to understanding the movement of Bigfoot in Ontario.

If you want to map where these creatures *live*, you study Sudbury, Temagami, Kenora, Thunder Bay.

If you want to map where they *move*, you study Muskoka.

What Muskoka Has Taught Me

More than any other southern or transitional region, Muskoka taught me to pay attention to the quiet places — not the dramatic ones.

1. Bigfoot uses geography the way wolves do — with strategy.

Ridge lines, swamps, waterways.
Muskoka is full of these.

2. Movement leaves smaller signs than territory.

Muskoka sightings are brief because the creatures aren't staying — they're traveling.

3. Silence matters.

The Muskoka Silence Phenomenon is a real field marker.

4. Human activity doesn't diminish presence — it shapes it.

Creatures thrive when humans concentrate along shorelines.
They simply move inland.

5. The deepest wilderness isn't always far from people.

Muskoka's interior can be as wild as anything north of Sudbury.

6. These creatures are more adaptive than most researchers admit.

They navigate around cottage country and busy roads without difficulty.

Muskoka is the wilderness that pretends to be tamed.
A region where the forests behind the cottages hold more mystery than people expect.

And in those silent forests, where the land presses in close and the lakes lie dark under the cedar shadows, something tall and old still walks — not staying long, but always passing through.

A quiet traveler.
A watcher.
A creature that belongs to the deeper north but moves through Muskoka as if it has always known the way.

Because it has.

CHAPTER 15 — KAWARTHA LAKES: THE SHADOWS ALONG THE TRAILS

Kawartha Lakes is one of those regions that fools people.

On a map, it looks friendly — cottages, fishing lodges, scenic highways, small towns built around warm lakes with names that feel familiar even if you've never been there. Bobcaygeon. Fenelon Falls. Lindsay. Kinmount. Buckhorn. Stony Lake. Places people go for weddings, boat rentals, ice cream, and sunsets.

But step a few kilometers off the paved roads and the truth shows itself:

Kawartha Lakes is wild.
Wild in ways southern Ontarians don't expect.
Wild in ways most visitors never see.

Behind the lakes are endless tracts of hardwood, swamp, cedar bog, old logging roads, and vast stretches of unbroken forest leading into Haliburton, Hastings, Durham, Algonquin, and even down toward Peterborough County.

This is a region of corridors — natural highways for wildlife.
And where corridors converge, creatures move.

Kawartha Lakes is not a hotspot like Temagami or Sudbury, but it is a concentration zone — a place where movement from several regions converges, and where sightings tend to cluster around edges, transitions, and the deep interior.

And the most important thing about this region?

The encounters that happen here feel close — closer than most people are comfortable admitting.

The Land That Doesn't Announce Itself

People think Kawartha Lakes is "cottage country lite." But the deeper forests tell a different story.

This region contains:

- old logging corridors
- deep hardwood stands
- cedar swamps that block sound
- countless small lakes only reachable by ATV or canoe
- thick forest belts between farmland
- abandoned homesteads and forgotten trails
- large stretches of crown land with almost no human presence
- wildlife densities that rival more northern districts

The Kawartha terrain is a mix of:

- swamp
- rock
- ridge

- forest
- marsh
- lake
- tangled underbrush

If you had to design terrain for a stealth-based, highly adaptive primate to move freely, Kawartha Lakes would fit the blueprint perfectly.

And that's exactly what multiple encounters suggest.

Ongoing Activity — The Kawartha Corridor (Case 142-13)

Prints found. Patterns emerging. Something moving through.

One of the most well-documented Kawartha Lakes cases involves a family who had persistent activity on their property — activity investigated by researchers who spent an entire day and night on-site.

The family reported:

- fresh tracks in soft earth
- repeated knocking sounds after dusk
- a sense of being watched from the treeline
- nighttime movement just beyond the property line

- periodic vocalizations, low and resonant
- dogs reacting strongly but refusing to approach the woods

The tracks were:

- large (15–16 inches)
- wide
- deep
- anatomically correct
- arranged in a staggered, bipedal gait

Investigators documented the prints, the terrain, and the spacing between steps — all consistent with a large biped. No hoax signs. No bear misidentification.

The family wasn't frightened — just confused.

They described the activity as "quiet but curious," almost as if something was passing through their area regularly, using the property as a waypoint.

This fits the pattern for Kawartha Lakes:

Creatures aren't living here.
They are traveling here.

And the property sits along one of the major travel corridors.

South of Sunderland — The Marsh Tracks (Case 139-12)

Tracks in a marsh. No human trail. No explanation.

Near Sunderland, south of Kawartha Lakes but within its ecological reach, a set of tracks was found deep within a marsh system. The witness reported:

- long, flat impressions
- deep toe marks
- a stride too long for a human
- no signs of sinkholes or hoax boards
- no human footprints leading to or from the tracks

The marsh was remote — the kind you avoid unless you have hip waders or a reason to be there.

No human would casually walk through this terrain.

But something did.

This part of the region is a corridor between Durham, Kawartha Lakes, and deeper systems to the north. The marsh tracks support the idea that something moves along the wetland belts instead of open forest — an intelligent choice for concealment.

Kawartha Behaviour Patterns

After analyzing all credible cases from the region, several behavioural patterns stand out:

1. Edge Habitat Movement

Creatures remain in forest edges, rarely crossing into open farmland.

2. Tracks in Mud, Sand, or Marsh

More track finds here than sightings, likely due to dense cover.

3. Nocturnal Activity

Most incidents occur between 10 p.m. and 4 a.m.

4. Silent Movement

Near-total silence during movement — unusual for moose or deer.

5. Curiosity Without Confrontation

A watchful presence, not aggressive, not territorial — passing through.

6. Corridor Use

Movement aligns with:

- forest belts
- lake chains
- swamp systems

- ridgeline trails
- abandoned roads

7. High Deer Density

A major attractant — Kawartha Lakes is deer-rich and predator-light, perfect for large omnivores.

Together, these patterns point to Kawartha as a seasonal or transitional habitat.

A place where creatures don't stay long — but pass through often.

The Kawartha Lakes Silence Effect

Like Muskoka, Kawartha Lakes has its own version of the silence phenomenon.

Witnesses repeatedly describe:

- birds stopping
- insects going quiet
- unnatural stillness
- a sudden change in the air
- the feeling of being watched
- then, movement in the brush
- or a low vocalization

- or a distant knock

This silence isn't wind-driven or weather-related.
It often appears minutes before an encounter.

Creatures in this region show a heightened awareness of human presence — they quiet the woods before revealing any sign of themselves.

This level of control appears almost intentional.

Why Kawartha Lakes Matters

It would be easy to dismiss Kawartha Lakes as "too domesticated" to support Bigfoot activity.

But that's the false picture people get from driving Highway 35 or 121.

The real Kawartha Lakes — the interior — is:

- wild
- thick
- isolated
- understudied
- interconnected

And strategically, it matters more than almost any other southern region.

1. It links Muskoka to Durham.

The southern migration route.

2. It links Algonquin to Hastings County.

The eastern migration route.

3. It links Haliburton to Simcoe County.

The western route into Georgian Bay corridors.

4. It contains massive swamp belts.

Perfect for concealment.

5. It has high deer density.

A primary food supply.

6. It has winter shelter zones.

Cedar lowlands are ideal for protection.

Kawartha Lakes is not a peripheral area — it is a hub.

A place where movement from multiple regions converges.

And where sightings accumulate quietly, consistently, and convincingly.

The Greater Kawartha Connection

Many Ontario researchers now believe Kawartha Lakes is not a standalone region, but part of a larger ecological cluster that includes:

- Durham County
- Haliburton
- Hastings County
- Peterborough County
- Muskoka South
- Simcoe East

Together, they form a nearly unbroken stretch of:

- forest
- marsh
- cedar
- ridges
- lakes
- deep bush

This corridor may serve as a seasonal migration path for one or more Bigfoot populations.

If creatures move between Algonquin and the southern counties, Kawartha Lakes is unavoidable.

And the sightings reflect that.

What Kawartha Lakes Has Taught Me

Kawartha Lakes is a reminder that wilderness does not have to be extreme, remote, or untouched to hide something big.

It only has to be connected.

And Kawartha Lakes is one of the most connected wilderness systems in southern Ontario.

It taught me:

1. Movement corridors matter as much as hotspots.

Creatures don't just live somewhere — they travel between places.

2. Quiet regions can hold big secrets.

Kawartha Lakes is subtle, but active.

3. The land between lakes is more important than the lakes themselves.

The deep interior is where the real mystery lies.

4. Not every sighting is dramatic — but patterns are.

Kawartha Lakes has some of the strongest patterns in the province.

5. These creatures might understand terrain better than we do.

They choose the exact corridors a stealth-based predator would.

Kawartha Lakes is not a place of roaring encounters or dramatic confrontations.
It is a place where the forest watches quietly from behind the maples and cedars — where something moves at night with purpose, familiarity, and the confidence of a creature that has been using these corridors for generations.

A shadow that comes and goes.
A whisper on the trails.
A presence in the darkness between lakes.

CHAPTER 16 — HALIBURTON: WHERE THE FOREST BREATHES DIFFERENTLY

Haliburton is a place where the wilderness changes its tone.

It isn't loud like Sudbury, where creatures throw rocks at lakes and hammer trees in deep valleys.
It isn't ancient and oppressive like Temagami, where the old growth feels aware of you.
It isn't expansive like Algonquin, where the land seems to swallow entire stories whole.

Haliburton's wilderness is something else:

Quiet. Heavy. Watchful. Intimate.

A landscape of steep ridges, black lakes, moss-cushioned floors, and white pine stands that block the sun even at noon. It's a place where the forest grows close around you — not to trap you, but to remind you that you're walking in someone else's hallway.

Locals say that Haliburton is the place where the wind changes, where the temperature drops five degrees for no reason, where you can be one minute from a highway but feel like you're ten kilometers deep in bush.

It's a region of isolation hidden behind tourism.
And in that isolation, people have seen things.
Heard things.
Felt things.

Haliburton is not the first region people name when they talk about Ontario Bigfoot hotspots.
But maybe it should be.

Because the things that happen here — the stories people tell in quiet voices, the tracks found in deep moss, the figures crossing ridgelines, the heavy steps near remote cabins — all follow patterns consistent with the province's strongest wilderness encounters.

Haliburton isn't a minor chapter in the mystery.
It's a bridge between the north and south — a place where movement, territory, and behaviour collide.

And some of the sightings from this region are among the most compelling in southern Ontario.

The Forests That Hold Their Own Secrets

To understand Haliburton, you need to understand the land:

- ancient granite ridges
- deep cedar swamps
- cold kettle lakes
- endless crown land
- thick corridors of undeveloped forest
- old logging roads choked by alder and maple
- valleys that swallow sound

- peaks that offer 20 km views

This is not "cottage country," no matter what people think when they see a summer map.

Drive five minutes off County Road 21 or 35 into the interior and the world becomes older. Wilder. Darker.

The ecosystem here is nearly identical to that of:

- Algonquin
- eastern Muskoka
- northern Kawartha
- western Hastings

All four of those regions have credible sightings. Haliburton sits directly in their overlap.

A creature moving between territories — especially one that uses ridgelines, creeks, and lake chains — would absolutely use Haliburton as a passage and potentially a seasonal refuge.

And the evidence suggests exactly that.

Haliburton's Confirmed & Credible Sightings

We start with the case that stands out most clearly.

171-14 — West of Carnarvon: Ongoing Activity Noticed by Residents

The woods that didn't stay quiet

Near Carnarvon — a place of lakes, swampy back valleys, and long stretches of unmanaged forest — multiple residents have reported ongoing strange activity.

Not one incident.
Not one night.
But repeated events over time, including:

- deep howls after midnight
- wood knocks heard from different directions
- heavy movement behind properties
- dogs reacting with fear instead of aggression
- sudden silence in areas normally full of sound
- fresh tree snaps on ridge trails
- tracks appearing after early winter snowfalls

This isn't tourist territory — it's quiet, rural, deep interior.

And the pattern is one I've seen again and again across the province:
ongoing, low-level activity in an area with perfect habitat and low human presence.

This is the hallmark of a migratory corridor or a seasonal feeding zone.

And Haliburton has many.

The Carnarvon Ridge — A Natural Highway

There is something special about the ridgeline west of Carnarvon:

- it stretches north–south for kilometers
- it connects directly to deeper systems on both sides
- it acts as a watershed divide
- the forest is thick, old, and nearly unbroken
- visibility from the top is excellent
- sound travels differently
- access routes are minimal

Hunters have reported hearing:

- heavy bipedal steps behind them
- long, low moans echoing through valleys
- sudden silence before dusk
- movement paralleling trails but staying hidden

One hunter described hearing a step that was "too heavy to be a deer and too coordinated to be a moose," followed by a sharp crack from a branch at shoulder height.

This is the exact type of behaviour commonly reported in Algonquin and west of Sudbury — regions with documented long-term presence.

Haliburton's Carnarvon Ridge may be more important than anyone has realized.

The Hidden Corridors

Haliburton contains several natural routes that a large, intelligent animal would use:

1. The Boshkung–Carnarvon Corridor

Dense swamp chains mixed with hardwood slopes.

2. The Kennisis–Redstone Interior Lakes

Remote, almost entirely surrounded by crown land.

3. The Haliburton Forest & Wildlife Reserve

Huge, privately managed wilderness with minimal human disturbance for most of the year.

4. The Kawagama–Kimball Lake Backcountry

A nearly unbroken stretch of wildland connecting toward Algonquin.

5. The Minden–Irondale Highlands

Rugged, steep, low-population ridges ideal for concealment.

Each corridor links to another region with sightings.

This is not coincidence.

Haliburton is less a home range and more a meeting place — a crossroads between major wilderness systems.

And the sightings reflect that.

Tracks Found After the First Snowfall

One of the most interesting Haliburton reports involves early winter tracks:

- 14–16 inches long
- flat, human-like
- deep heel impressions
- clear toe splay
- spaced far apart in a straight line
- moving from swamp to ridge without deviation

The witness who found them was a trapper — someone with decades of experience in reading ground sign. He dismissed:

- bear
- moose

- elk
- wolves
- human pranksters

No known animal in Ontario makes bipedal prints of that size with that gait.

The trapper described the stride as:

"long, confident, and deliberate — something walking like it had somewhere to go."

This matches patterns seen in:

- Sudbury
- Thunder Bay
- Cochrane
- Kenora

Where creatures move long distances using natural land formations.

Haliburton's interior ridges are perfect for this.

Night Sounds in the Highlands

Multiple cottage owners and seasonal residents have reported nighttime sounds that fall into three categories:

1. Heavy, slow pacing outside cabins

Not deer — too heavy.
Not bear — too precise.
Not moose — too quiet.

2. Sharp wood knocks echoing across lakes

Single knocks.
Double knocks.
Rare triple patterns.

3. Long, rising howls heard across valleys

Not coyotes — too deep.
Not wolves — too human-like.
Not dogs — too long.

One witness heard a howl so deep it vibrated inside the cabin walls. Another described hearing something walking in the brush behind their property "on two legs, not four."

The consistency across decades is striking.

Why Haliburton Is a Perfect Habitat

Haliburton offers everything a reclusive, intelligent animal would need:

1. Food Sources

- deer

- beaver
- fish
- seasonal berries
- roots
- maple buds
- small game

2. Cover

- swamp belts
- dense hardwood
- deep cedar thickets
- hemlock valleys

3. Terrain Advantage

Ridge systems allow easy movement and line-of-sight control.

4. Low Human Density

Especially outside summer and fall.

5. Water Everywhere

Creeks, lakes, bogs — water in all directions.

6. Year-Round Viability

Cedar lowlands offer snow shelter.
Ridges offer wind breaks.
Interior lakes freeze slowly.

7. Escape Routes

Multiple wilderness exits in every direction.

Haliburton is not just habitable — it's ideal.

Connections to Adjacent Sightings

When you map sightings by ecological corridor instead of political region, Haliburton's role becomes obvious:

- Activity in Kawartha Lakes flows northwest into Haliburton.

- Activity in Algonquin flows southwest toward Haliburton's ridge systems.

- Activity in Muskoka flows east into Haliburton's hardwood belt.

- Activity in Hastings County flows west along the York River valley.

- Haliburton's southern areas connect directly into Durham County tracks and knocks.

Haliburton is the center of the wheel.

If these creatures move seasonally or territorially, Haliburton is unavoidable.

And the patterns support exactly that.

Personal Observations from the Region

While I haven't had a major encounter in Haliburton, I have spent enough time in the region to know that the forest *behaves differently* here.

Things I have personally noticed over the years:

- mornings where the forest goes silent as if something moved through before I arrived
- ridge systems that offer too perfect of a vantage point
- cedar swamps that feel active even when still
- tracks of moose and deer suddenly ending near deeper water
- faint knocks on distant lakes at dusk
- the sense of being watched along unused trails

Haliburton is not just scenic.
It's alive.

The land feels aware.
Not hostile — just watchful.
Like something has claimed it for longer than we've been here.

And that something still walks its valleys.

What Haliburton Has Taught Me

Haliburton is a reminder that Ontario's mystery isn't confined to remote northern landscapes.
It thrives in transitional regions — places that connect, overlap, and merge.

Haliburton taught me:

1. Movement corridors reveal more than hotspots.

The creatures that move between regions may be more important than the ones that stay put.

2. Silence is a sign.

The Haliburton Silence Effect mirrors patterns in Muskoka, Kawartha, and parts of Algonquin.

3. Terrain shapes behaviour.

Haliburton's steep ridges create perfect ambush and observation points — ideal for a creature that prefers not to be seen.

4. Multiple sightings across decades indicate consistency.

Patterns in Carnarvon and the surrounding lakes never fully stopped.

5. Wilderness doesn't need to be enormous to be powerful.

Haliburton has fewer people than Muskoka and less fame than Algonquin — but its interior is just as wild.

6. This region may hold knowledge about migration.

Creatures use it as a pass, a refuge, a seasonal route.

Haliburton is the place where Ontario's mystery tightens — where something large moves with an ease that only comes from long familiarity.

A creature that walks the ridges at night.
A shadow in the cedar stands.
A watcher moving between worlds.

Haliburton isn't just another region on the map.
It's part of the spine of Ontario's wilderness — and it carries that weight.

And if the deeper north is the heart of the mystery,
then Haliburton is one of its most important arteries.

CHAPTER 17 — HASTINGS COUNTY: THE HIDDEN PATHWAYS OF THE EASTERN SHIELD

Hastings County sits in the middle of Ontario like a hinge — connecting the deeper, older wilderness of the Canadian Shield to the rolling agricultural country of the southeast. It's a place where granite ridges meet farmland, where the forest grows in thick belts, and where old logging roads disappear into cedar swamps that have barely changed since the 1800s.

People think of Hastings as quiet, rural, ordinary.

They're wrong.

The truth is that Hastings County is a wild corridor, a zone where the land funnels movement in ways most people never notice. It is one of the most strategically positioned wilderness regions in the province — linking Haliburton, Kawartha Lakes, Lennox & Addington, and the southeastern highlands in a way that creates perfect pathways for the kind of creature capable of traveling unseen.

And every few years, someone in Hastings County sees something they can't explain.

Something that steps out of the forest for a moment, crosses a path, reacts to a human cry, or presses a massive hand against the canvas wall of a tent.

Hastings doesn't have hundreds of sightings.
It has *important ones*.

Rare, but convincing.
Quiet, but consistent.

The kind of sightings that make you look at the landscape differently when you drive through it.

Because once you know what you're looking at, you realize how easy it would be for something big, quiet, and intelligent to move through here unnoticed.

And how often it may have already done so.

The Land That Controls Movement

Hastings County contains one of the most overlooked wilderness structures in Ontario:
a long, rugged, forested corridor running from Tweed → Bancroft → Maynooth and into the deeper highlands toward Algonquin's southeast.

This corridor includes:

- thick cedar swamps
- ridges of exposed granite
- stands of old-growth hemlock
- maple valleys rich with deer
- surprisingly remote lakes
- abandoned farm lots returning to forest

- forgotten ATV trails

- river systems with heavy brush cover

This land directs wildlife — not just deer and coyotes, but anything larger.

If you gave a military strategist the task of choosing the most concealed route across eastern Ontario, they'd pick the same pathways that wildlife — and possibly something bigger — already use.

And right along that route are the region's best sightings.

Case 163-13 — Near Tweed: The Trail-Side Giant

A witness sees a massive ape-like figure on a trail

Near Tweed, a witness walking a backwoods trail on a summer day saw something that did not match any wildlife known to the region.

The figure:

- stood upright

- had broad shoulders

- was covered in dark hair

- moved with a smooth, powerful stride

- crossed the trail in two or three steps

- disappeared into dense bush without sound

The witness described it as "an ape — but not an ape," something far larger, more deliberate, and more aware.

They froze.
The creature didn't.

What's striking is not just what the witness saw, but *where* they saw it:

- along a corridor linking Tweed to deeper forest
- near a ridge system that runs for dozens of kilometers
- close to wetlands where deer feed in early summer
- in an area with few permanent residents

This is exactly where a creature passing through would reveal itself briefly — just long enough to be seen when the terrain forces it across a trail.

And exactly the type of sighting that happens in regions known for legitimate activity.

Case 147-88 — Near Foxboro: The Tent Incident

A child's memory of a creature pushing its massive hands against the tent

The Foxboro case is one of the most disturbing from the region — not because of violence, but because of proximity.

In 1988, a ten-year-old child camping with family heard something approaching in the night.

Not walking.
Running.

Heavy footsteps circled their tent.
Branches snapped under weight.
Then — the part no one forgets:

Two large hands pressed against the canvas wall of the tent.

Large enough to create full impressions.
High enough to suggest a creature taller than a grown man.
Strong enough to distort the fabric.

The family screamed.
Something ran off into the woods, crashing through brush with long strides.

The next morning:

- impressions were found around the tent

- no bear tracks were present

- no claw marks

- no signs of typical bear investigation behaviour

The child never forgot it.
And as an adult, they still refuse to camp in that part of Hastings County.

This case suggests something bold moved through — something comfortable approaching human structures, but quick to retreat when alarmed.

It's one of the clearest human-proximity incidents in southeastern Ontario.

Other Activity Across the Region

While the two main cases stand out for clarity and detail, Hastings County has smaller incidents that create a stronger pattern when viewed as a whole:

1. Unexplained vocalizations

Several families living on rural properties have reported:

- long, rising howls
- deep moans
- nighttime vocal exchanges across valleys
- sudden silences after calling deer

These are *not* coyote or fox sounds.

Multiple witnesses described the vocals as:

"Something with a chest… something huge."

2. Large tracks found near wetlands

Hunters and hikers have reported:

- long, flat footprints
- deep heel impressions

- toe splay in soft mud
- wide step spacing

These prints often appear after rainstorms or during early thaw.

3. Heavy biped movement

Witnesses describe:

- two-legged cadence
- heavy ground impact
- slower pace than deer
- deliberate steps instead of bounding

Several described the sense that the creature "paralleled" them from within the treeline.

4. Tree snaps at shoulder height

In Hastings, tree snaps are often found:

- 6–8 feet above ground
- with fresh splintering
- in clusters near ridge trails

These are consistent with territorial markers documented in northern hotspots.

5. Strange nighttime pacing near camps and cabins

Families report pacing outside:

- hunting camps
- remote cottages
- cabins near old logging trails

Often accompanied by silence, then slow retreat.

Together, these incidents form a mosaic — a pattern of movement, behaviour, and presence.

And all of it matches the larger Bigfoot profile seen across Ontario.

Why Hastings County Fits the Pattern

Hastings provides five key elements that explain its recurring activity:

1. It is a perfect natural corridor.

Creatures moving from:

- Kawartha
- Haliburton
- Algonquin
- Lennox & Addington

would pass through Hastings.

The terrain funnels movement.

2. It has low human density.

Large swaths of Hastings are sparsely populated or seasonal-only.

3. It has food.

Deer are abundant.
Beavers fill many streams.
Berries and mast crops are plentiful.

4. It has cover year-round.

Cedar swamps provide perfect winter concealment.

5. It has silence.

Certain valleys in Hastings absorb sound so well that an animal could move silently at close range.

This combination makes Hastings one of the most viable southern-to-northern migration routes in the province.

The Tweed Connection — A Hidden Hotspot?

In recent years, multiple researchers have quietly noted that the area around Tweed seems to produce sightings that resemble:

- Durham County
- Kawartha Lakes

- Haliburton Highlands
- Northern Lennox & Addington

It sits at the convergence of several movement pathways:

- the Skootamatta River
- the Black River
- the Moira River
- multiple creek systems
- old trapper roads and ATV trails
- the hardwood ridges near Hungerford and Thomasburg

These corridors make Tweed a natural funnel for wildlife.

And exactly the kind of terrain where a large biped could slip through unnoticed — emerging only when the land forces it across a trail.

Which is exactly what happened in Case 163-13.

A Region of Quiet Encounters

Hastings County is not dramatic like Sudbury.
It's not eerie like Muskoka.
It's not overwhelming like Temagami.

Its encounters are subtler:

- a flash of movement

- a call echoing across a valley at dusk
- a track found in an impossible location
- heavy footsteps stopping just outside a tent
- tree knocks answered from deep forest
- a presence watching from ridgelines

This subtlety is part of why the region is overlooked.

But subtle does not mean insignificant.

In fact, subtle often means *passing through* — and passing through is exactly what makes Hastings important.

Because movement is the key to understanding Bigfoot patterns in Ontario.

What Hastings County Has Taught Me

Hastings taught me to respect the quiet places.

The places people overlook.
The places they drive through on the way to "real wilderness."
The places where the land feels unassuming — until it isn't.

From Hastings I learned:

1. Major activity often hides in minor regions.

Small sightings can connect bigger patterns.

2. A few strong cases matter more than dozens of vague ones.

The Foxboro and Tweed cases are central pillars.

3. There are still vast pockets of wilderness in southeastern Ontario.

More than most people realize.

4. Creatures may use Hastings as a seasonal travel route.

Its corridors match typical migratory behaviour.

5. Silence means something.

Many witnesses in Hastings describe pre-encounter silence — consistent with high-tier sightings.

6. Hastings might be part of a larger, poorly recognized hotspot.

A cluster including Tweed, Denbigh, Bancroft, and the Haliburton edge.

Hastings County may not dominate the news.
It may not have dozens of famous cases.

But it is a critical piece of the provincial puzzle — a place where the shadows move between larger territories, where trails tell stories, and where the forest shows just enough to remind you something big is still out there.

Something that walks.
Something that watches.
Something passing through the hidden pathways of the eastern Shield.

CHAPTER 18 — LENNOX & ADDINGTON: THE BORDERLANDS OF THE EASTERN WILD

Lennox & Addington is one of the strangest regions in Ontario.

Not because of loud encounters.
Not because of dramatic sightings.
Not because of long-term hotspots like Sudbury or Temagami.

It's strange because of where it sits.

A borderland.
A seam between worlds.
A place where the rocky Canadian Shield collides with rolling farmland and deep, silent lakes that sit like dark mirrors under the pines.

Half north.
Half south.
Not quite wilderness, not quite settled.

But the land here has an uncanny, unsettled feel — especially in the interior stretches between Cloyne, Kaladar, Denbigh, Flinton, and the Puzzle Lake area. These are places where the Shield breaks through the ground, where the forest is thick and tangled, where old homesteads sit half-swallowed by moss, and where lakes have no cottages, no trails, no noise — nothing but the sound of loons and the slow drip of water off granite.

It is here, in this quiet borderland, that some of the most unnerving signs of Sasquatch activity in southeastern Ontario have been found.

Not many sightings.
But *good* sightings.
The kind with detail, fear, and physical evidence.

The kind that stay with people.

The Puzzle Lake Boulder Incident (Case 149-13)

The lake that threw something back

Puzzle Lake is a strange place.

Remote.
Hard to reach.
Surrounded by tangled forest and granite outcrops that feel ancient in a way few places in southern Ontario do.

In July of 2013, a kayaker entered a narrow channel off Puzzle Lake — a quiet place where cattails brushed the hull and dragonflies weaved across the air.

It was peaceful.

Until it wasn't.

Without warning, a massive boulder — not a rock, not a stone, but a *boulder* — crashed into the water only meters behind the kayak. The splash was so violent that water sprayed over the witness's shoulders.

The kayaker turned, expecting to see:

- a bear on a cliff

- a person

- a collapsed piece of rock

But there was nothing.

Just the ripples.
Just the widening rings.
Just the silence returning.

The boulder was later estimated to weigh at least 60–80 pounds.

No animal in this region, except a human, could have thrown it.
And no human was there.

Puzzle Lake has always had an eerie reputation among locals — a place where people hear pacing on shore at night, where dogs refuse to leave campsites, and where something large moves in the treeline without being seen.

The boulder incident was not the first report.
And it would not be the last.

The Denbigh–Flinton Corridor

The forgotten backcountry where things still wander

The stretch between Denbigh, Flinton, Cloyne, and Kaladar is one of the least-discussed wilderness areas in southern Ontario.

It is also one of the most important.

This interior region contains:

- abandoned logging routes
- thick hemlock valleys
- unbroken tracts of crown land
- unmanaged lakes
- large cedar swamps
- exposed granite ridges
- minimal permanent population

It is a major wildlife corridor connecting:

- Hastings County
- Algonquin's southeastern drainages
- Bon Echo backcountry
- Lennox & Addington's lake clusters
- North Frontenac's dark-sky wilderness

This is a perfect movement route for a large, stealthy animal.

And people who live near this corridor report:

- deep knocks in the forest at dusk
- long, rising moans late at night
- heavy footsteps around remote cabins

- strange pacing outside tents
- deer suddenly evacuating an area
- silence that drops like a curtain in certain valleys

No single event screams "Bigfoot."
But the patterns make more sense when viewed through that lens.

These are not random noises.
They're coordinated.
Consistent.
Predictable.

And on rare occasions, they become something far more intense.

Heavy Footsteps at Night — The Addington Dark Walk

One of the most compelling cases from the region comes from a pair of campers near an unnamed lake south of Cloyne.

They were camped off-trail — deep enough that no one should have been there unless they were deliberately bushwhacking into backcountry.

Just after midnight, they heard heavy, deliberate, bipedal footsteps approaching their camp.

Not from the water.
Not from the ridge.
From the dark woods behind the tent.

Each step:

- slow
- heavy
- carefully placed
- too measured to be a bear
- too spaced to be deer
- too weighty to be a person

The pacing stopped just behind the tent.

Then came the breathing.

Low.
Slow.
Wet.
Deep enough to vibrate the tent fabric.

The couple froze, not daring to move.

After perhaps thirty seconds — though it felt like minutes — the footsteps turned and retreated with the same slow, heavy cadence.

No vocalization.
No bluff charge.
No curiosity.
Just steady movement away, like something inspecting the area, confirming the presence of humans, then leaving.

This behaviour is consistent with dozens of close-range encounters documented in Ontario's north.

Whatever moved through that camp behaved like a large, cautious, intelligent animal.

The kind that prefers not to be seen.

The Belleville–Napanee Edge Cases

Although most of Lennox & Addington's wilderness lies north, the southern region has its own quiet pattern:

Reports near the:

- Salmon River
- Napanee River
- Varty Lake wetlands
- Moscow–Enterprise corridor
- Camden East backcountry

These are not dramatic sightings — just brief, unsettling encounters:

- something large, dark, and upright crossing a rural road at dusk
- a sudden, powerful tree knock from deep swamp
- dogs becoming terrified on forest walks
- deer stampeding from sections of ridge for no apparent reason

- heavy biped movement at night near campgrounds

These "border sightings" often get dismissed because they happen so close to settled areas.

But they shouldn't be.

These were once the most heavily forested regions in all of southeastern Ontario.
And many of the ridges and wetlands still hold that character — wild, silent, undisturbed.

Perfect habitat.

Lennox & Addington Behaviour Patterns

After compiling all known reports — official and unofficial — clear behavioural patterns emerge:

1. Proximity Without Confrontation

Creatures here approach camps or kayaks but pull away when discovered.

2. Water-Focused Movement

Most events occur near lakes, narrow channels, or swamp corridors.

3. Ridge-Line Crossings

Sightings occur at ridge transitions where movement is briefly exposed.

4. Nighttime Dominance

Every high-quality encounter occurs between 11 p.m. and 4 a.m.

5. Boulder or Rock Throws

The Puzzle Lake case stands out as one of Ontario's most extreme examples.

6. Silence Phenomenon

Witnesses consistently report sudden stillness before an encounter.

7. Seasonal Presence

Evidence suggests spring and summer activity — especially during high deer movement and fish runs.

These patterns resemble activity in Hastings County, Haliburton, and Peterborough regions — forming part of a larger southeastern behavioural cluster.

The Wilderness People Forget Exists

If someone asked which Ontario regions contain true wilderness, most would say:

- Algonquin
- Temagami
- Quetico

- Sudbury
- Thunder Bay

Almost no one says Lennox & Addington.

But they should.

The northern half of the county contains:

- enormous crown land blocks
- unbroken forest belts
- low population density
- wildlife corridors extending into deeper Shield
- lakes only reachable by ATV or canoe
- terrain where GPS signals fail
- valleys where sound disappears

This is wilderness in every meaningful sense.

Quiet.
Old.
Undisturbed.

And something large can move through it without leaving more than a splash, a track, or a fading memory.

The Bon Echo Connection

North of Kaladar lies Bon Echo Provincial Park, one of Ontario's most spectacular geological features — massive cliff faces rising over Mazinaw Lake, ancient pictographs, and deep interior forest.

The park connects to the same granite and hemlock wilderness stretching west toward Flinton and east toward Cloyne.

Campers in the deeper sections of Bon Echo have quietly reported:

- long, deep howls at night
- heavy pacing through cedar swamps
- knocks echoing against the cliffs
- something large moving along ridge trails after dark

These reports rarely reach official channels because most occur in the shoulder seasons — spring and fall — when the park is quiet, and the people who hear them don't connect what they heard with the Bigfoot phenomenon.

But the behaviour is unmistakable.

Bon Echo may be one of the least-discussed Bigfoot-adjacent areas in Ontario.
And yet, everything about it supports that possibility.

What Lennox & Addington Has Taught Me

This region taught me that wilderness is not just about size — it's about connection.

Lennox & Addington is not as vast as Algonquin or as dramatic as Temagami.
But what it *has* is just as important:

1. A network of wild corridors.

The region is a funnel between major habitats.

2. Silence that means something.

Multiple cases describe pre-encounter quiet.

3. Evidence of intelligence and caution.

No aggressive behaviour, only proximity and observation.

4. Lakes and swamps that hide more than they show.

Puzzle Lake, Mazinaw, and the interior ponds are perfect cover.

5. A habitat suited for seasonal travel.

The creatures may pass through annually.

6. A pattern matching neighbouring counties.

Hastings, Frontenac, and Haliburton all show similar signs.

Lennox & Addington is the threshold region — a place where something moves quietly, occasionally showing itself, always pulling away, leaving only enough behind to remind you that the wilderness doesn't end where the map says it should.

Something big walks these lakes.
Something that knows the terrain better than any of us.

Something that has used these corridors long before the roads came.

A shadow in the borderlands.
A creature of the granite and cedar.
A traveller of old pathways.

And it's still out there.

CHAPTER 19 — PETERBOROUGH COUNTY: THE LOWLAND SHADOWS OF THE LAND BETWEEN

Peterborough County is a region defined by thresholds — places where the land shifts from rolling farmland into granite, from warm southern ecosystems into the rugged beginnings of the Canadian Shield. It is part of what geologists call The Land Between, a transitional zone that stretches across Ontario like a fault line of old rock and deep forest.

It's a region that doesn't fully belong to the south
and doesn't fully belong to the north.

But it belongs to something.

Something that moves through forest belts at night.
Something that crosses quiet backroads without being seen.
Something that leaves tracks in soft mud beside dark rivers.
Something that howls across cold lakes in early spring.

Peterborough County isn't known as a Bigfoot hotspot.
That's exactly why its sightings matter.

They appear in unexpected places — farm edges, creek bottoms, conservation areas, and quiet lake chains — places where most people assume nothing unusual could survive.

But the creatures that move through Ontario's wilderness don't care about assumptions.

They care about corridors.

And Peterborough County has some of the most important wilderness corridors in southern Ontario.

The Land Between — Ontario's Secret Wilderness Spine

To understand Peterborough, you must understand the geography that defines it.

This region marks the shift between:

- limestone lowlands
- granite highlands
- small but dense lake clusters
- deep swamp networks
- high, forested ridges

It is a land shaped by:

- glacial scars
- misfit lakes
- cedar-choked valleys
- thick mixed forest
- rugged bedrock rises

- old logging routes sliding into disuse

On a map, Peterborough County looks populated.
In reality, the interior is a labyrinth — a maze of backroads, abandoned trails, and old homesteads that the forest has reclaimed.

There are hundreds of places here where you can walk a kilometer off a trail and find yourself in total silence, surrounded by terrain that feels more like Algonquin than southern Ontario.

And that's where the sightings begin.

The Lakefield Corridor

Where the Trent River becomes something older

The first pattern appears around Lakefield, where the Trent River narrows into shield-like terrain.

Locals have quietly reported:

- heavy, biped-like steps moving along the riverbank at night
- deep howls echoing across Katchewanooka Lake
- dogs refusing to enter the woods behind farm properties
- strange pacing sounds in the cedar stands near the water

One late-summer witness described hearing something walking just behind their rural property:

"Two legs. Heavy. Slow. Like a person wearing 200 pounds."

But no flashlight beam revealed anything.
And whatever it was, it stopped the moment the witness stepped outside — then resumed walking only when he retreated indoors.

This pattern — cautious approach, controlled movement — is typical of many transitional region encounters.

Something was listening.
Approaching.
Evaluating.

That behaviour appears again and again across the county.

The Warsaw Caves Region — A Hidden Wilderness

The Warsaw Caves Conservation Area is known for its unique karst landscape:

- underground rivers
- fractured limestone caverns
- thick forest
- ridges and cliffs
- deep silence

Locals and campers have reported:

- rock clacks from deep woods (consistent with knock patterns)

- low moans echoing through valleys

- stone throws landing near campsites at night

- heavy pacing along the forest edge of group campsites

One long-time ranger admitted privately:

"We hear things out here that aren't coyotes, and they're not humans. Some nights, the woods feel like they're watching you."

Karst terrain amplifies sound in unusual ways — but it doesn't *create* sounds.
Something has to be there to make them.

And multiple visitors have heard the same patterns across different years.

North of Buckhorn — The Roadside Figures

Between Buckhorn and the rugged east toward Anstruther Lake, several drivers have reported seeing:

- tall, dark silhouettes

- crossing rural roads at dusk

- moving quickly but smoothly

- stepping into forest without sound

One truck driver described seeing a dark, upright figure cross the asphalt "in three steps," heading toward a ridge that separates farm country from deep, shield forest.

He slowed down, expecting a bear.
But the figure never dropped to all fours.
Never hesitated.
Never turned.

Just walked — tall, deliberate, and impossibly fast for a human.

This sighting location matters:

That exact roadway sits at the meeting point of:

- Haliburton County
- Kawartha Highlands
- North Kawartha
- the interior lake chains

A natural funnel.

A common trait of Ontario roadside sightings is that they happen where terrain compresses movement — between a swamp and a cliff, between a river and a road, between two rising ridges.

This Buckhorn sighting fits that pattern flawlessly.

The Trent Lakes Cluster

The Trent Lakes region — north of Peterborough, east of Lake Simcoe, west of Buckhorn — hosts a series of quiet, uneasy events:

- strange whoops echoing across small lakes

- heavy steps heard behind seasonal cottages in May and June

- logs placed across ATV trails overnight

- deep, guttural breaths heard outside tents

- tree snaps high above human reach

Many of these are never reported officially.
Local residents shrug them off, call them "moose," "bears," or "somebody messing around."

But the details usually tell another story.

The breaths are too deep.
The steps too deliberate.
The tree snaps too high.

This is the kind of activity seen in Simcoe County, Durham, Kawartha Lakes, and other transitional regions.

A creature moving through the wilderness in a careful, observational pattern.

Why Peterborough County Works as a Bigfoot Corridor

There are reasons why a reclusive, intelligent primate could use Peterborough County:

1. Water Corridors

The region is full of:

- rivers
- streams
- wetland systems
- connected lake chains
- quiet shorelines

Bigfoot sightings across North America frequently occur along water systems.

Peterborough has dozens of such corridors.

2. Mixed Forest for Concealment

Black spruce.
Cedar.
Hardwood.
Thick underbrush.

Cover is everywhere.

3. Deer Abundance

The region is full of:

- white-tailed deer
- beaver
- small game
- berries

- maple buds
- aquatic plants

Food sources are plentiful.

4. Low Nighttime Human Presence

Cottages are seasonal.
Hiking is low after dusk.
Snowmobile routes empty by late winter.

Nighttime is almost entirely undisturbed.

5. Transition Terrain

Creatures moving between:

- Durham
- Kawartha
- Haliburton
- Hastings
- Muskoka

would all pass through Peterborough County at some point.

This is the literal center of the southern movement network.

The Behaviour Patterns in Peterborough County

After compiling all known sightings (official and unofficial), several patterns emerge:

1. Nighttime Movement

Almost all encounters occur between 10 p.m. and 3 a.m.

2. Ridge-Line Crossings

Figures appear where trails intersect ridges.

3. Observational Behaviour

Witnesses often feel watched before any sound occurs.

4. Subtle Vocalizations

Low moans or soft whoops are more common than full howls.

5. Water-Adjacent Evidence

Most tracks and noises occur within 200 meters of water.

6. Single Individuals

No family groups reported — consistent with transient travel.

7. Silence Before Activity

The "drop-off" in ambient sound appears in multiple accounts.

These patterns match transitional counties such as:

- Simcoe
- Durham
- Kawartha
- Hastings

Peterborough is part of that same migratory system.

The Strange Weight of the Land

One thing I've always noticed about Peterborough's interior is the feeling — the atmosphere — of the land.

Some forests feel empty.
Some forests feel alive.
Peterborough's forests feel… *aware*.

There are places near:

- Burleigh Falls
- Apsley
- Stony Lake
- Chandos Lake
- Nogies Creek
- Big Cedar Lake

...where the trees feel closer, the shadows longer, the silence deeper.

Places where you find yourself glancing over your shoulder for no logical reason.

Places where the land feels like it remembers things.

Even as a field researcher used to Temagami's pressure, Sudbury's force, and Algonquin's ancient weight — Peterborough's quiet intensity feels different.

Not aggressive.
Not hostile.

Just watchful.

Like something is always nearby,
but choosing not to show itself.

What Peterborough County Has Taught Me

Peterborough taught me that Bigfoot isn't limited to iconic wilderness.

It thrives in the in-between places — the forgotten backroads, the lake chains nobody paddles, the rivers with no trails beside them, the swamps people assume hold nothing larger than a moose.

Peterborough County taught me:

1. Transitional zones matter as much as hotspots.

Movement shapes sightings.

2. A lack of reports doesn't mean a lack of activity.

People don't expect to see Bigfoot here — so they don't report what they see.

3. Ridge and water systems funnel wildlife.

And likely funnel Bigfoot as well.

4. Quiet encounters can carry more weight than dramatic ones.

The subtle ones often reveal real presence.

5. The Land Between is a highway of wilderness.

A biological superhighway for large mammals.

6. Something uses this region with intent.

Careful.
Cautious.
Consistent.

Peterborough County is the quiet middle of Ontario's Bigfoot map — the place where shadows pass through, leaving only enough of themselves behind to remind you that the old wilderness rhythms have never truly stopped.

The roads are new.
The cottages are new.
The towns are new.

But the thing moving between those ridges
has been walking here much, much longer.

CHAPTER 20 — FRONTENAC COUNTY: THE DARK CORRIDORS OF THE SOUTHERN SHIELD

Frontenac County sits in one of the most underrated wildlands in Ontario.

Most people hear "Frontenac" and think of Kingston, the Rideau Canal, or farmland spreading south toward Lake Ontario. But that's the southern edge — the part people see. The real Frontenac lies north of Highway 7, where the land rises into granite, the lakes multiply, and the forest grows so thick and old you can walk an hour without hearing a car, a voice, or anything human at all.

Frontenac is part of what scientists call the Frontenac Arch, an ancient granite bridge connecting the Canadian Shield in Ontario to the Adirondacks in New York. It is one of the most important ecological corridors in eastern North America — a literal land bridge for wildlife movement between vast wilderness systems.

And if this creature — Bigfoot, Sasquatch, whatever name people choose — is real,
this is exactly the kind of corridor it would use.

Frontenac County is not famous for sightings.
But the ones that occur here carry weight.
They feel old.
They feel rooted.
They feel like echoes of something that has been walking this land for a long, long time.

Because in these forests — deep, black, silent forests — the past is never far away,
and the present feels thin.

The Wilderness People Don't Know Exists

North Frontenac, Central Frontenac, and much of Addington Highlands form one of the least understood wilderness zones south of Algonquin.

This region contains:

- enormous stretches of crown land

- deep swamps with no trails

- lakes accessible only by canoe

- old trapper cabins lost to moss

- ridges that run for kilometers

- forests so dense they block out daylight

- the largest dark-sky preserve in southern Ontario

Frontenac is, in many ways, a southern Algonquin — but without the crowds, without the traffic, without the noise.

If you dropped someone blindfolded into the interior of North Frontenac, they could believe they were 100 miles inside Temagami.

And that's where the sightings happen.

Not on the highways.
Not near cottages.
But in the black heart of the forest — the places the map barely acknowledges.

The Sharbot Lake–Ardoch Corridor

Low reports, high credibility

Around Sharbot Lake, Ardoch, and Mississippi Station, there have been decades of quiet, whispered accounts from locals:

- heavy, two-legged footsteps pacing camps at night
- long, low moans echoing across narrow lakes
- sudden "dead zones" where the forest falls silent
- strange, tree-shaking impacts far from any trail
- tall, dark figures stepping between trees at dusk

Nothing sensational.
Nothing wild.
Just the same patterns repeated quietly over generations.

One cottager north of Ardoch reported that during the early 2000s, something large "walked circles around our tent platform for over an hour." They heard:

- two-legged cadence
- incredibly heavy footfalls

- breaths pausing between steps

- no vocalization

- no retreat until first light

The next morning revealed nothing except a feeling the witnesses couldn't shake:

"Whatever it was, it wasn't a person.
And it was checking us out."

This type of behaviour — slow circling, quiet monitoring — matches patterns from Algonquin, Haliburton, and Hastings.

Creatures here do not confront.
They watch.

The Frontenac Provincial Park Incidents

Deep interior encounters in one of the darkest parks in Ontario

Frontenac Provincial Park is a backcountry-only wilderness.
No car camping.
No quick access.
Just:

- long trails

- quiet lakes

- interior campsites

- dense forest

- complete silence

Hikers and canoeists have quietly reported:

1. Heavy pacing behind their campsites

Footsteps moving parallel to the treeline, slow and deliberate.

2. Tree knocks in early morning hours

Single strikes, followed seconds later by distant replies.

3. Long, low calls echoing across interior lakes

Witnesses often describe these as "too long and too deep" to be coyotes.

4. Sudden forest silence

Owls stop.
Crickets stop.
Frogs stop.
The woods go still.

One backcountry paddler described hearing a single, thunderous tree knock echo across Birch Lake at 5 a.m. The lake was completely calm. Mist rising. No wind. No campers on the opposite shore.

A few minutes later, a second knock came from deeper forest behind them.

Then silence.

This is not camping folklore — this is consistent behaviour recorded across Ontario.

The Plevna–Ompah Ridge System

A natural superhighway

North of Plevna and Ompah lies one of the wildest stretches of the entire region:

- multi-kilometer ridges
- interconnected wetlands
- deep beaver meadows
- old logging roads reclaimed by alder
- enormous stretches with no houses, cottages, or lights
- endless protected land

This terrain resembles parts of Sudbury and Temagami on a smaller scale — rugged, harsh, and almost completely unpopulated.

Hunters in this region have reported:

- branch breaks at 7–8 feet
- long, spaced strides in wet moss
- "shadow figures" crossing ridge crests at dusk
- moose vacating valleys suddenly
- heavy, bipedal steps paralleling trails

One hunter described it perfectly:

"There's something in those ridges.
Something big.
Something that knows its way better than we ever will."

Frontenac's interior ridges function exactly like Temagami's:

- vantage points
- movement corridors
- safe observation areas
- minimal human disturbance

A creature using these ridges could travel 30–40 km without being seen.

Why Frontenac County Works as Habitat

Frontenac offers almost everything the creature needs:

1. Food Supply

- deer
- beaver
- fish
- berries
- maple buds

- amphibians
- roots

2. Concealment

- cedar swamps
- thick hardwood
- hemlock valleys
- tangled underbrush

3. Terrain Advantage

Ridges for visibility.
Swamps for stealth.
Mixed forest for movement.

4. Continuity

It connects Algonquin → Hastings → Lennox & Addington → Adirondacks.

5. Low Population Density

Especially north of Highway 7.
Seasonal cottages empty from October–May.

6. Perfect Silence

Many valleys in Frontenac swallow sound.

7. Year-Round Viability

Shelter in cedar lowlands.
Frozen swamps allow easy winter movement.

This region is a stealth specialist's dream.

Behaviour Patterns Unique to Frontenac

Across all known sightings and reports, the Frontenac creature behaviour aligns with transitional regions (like Peterborough and Kawartha Lakes) but with a northern edge.

Patterns include:

1. Slow, deliberate pacing

Not rushing, not fleeing — just monitoring.

2. Sparse vocalizations

One or two long calls per night, never repeated.

3. Tree knocks as primary communication

More knocks here than howls.

4. High ridgeline movement

Creatures seen crossing ridge crests at dusk.

5. Swamp-edge tracks

Fresh impressions in soft ground after rain.

6. Proximity without confrontation

Approaching camps but keeping distance.

7. A sense of being watched

Witnesses consistently describe this feeling.

It's subtle.
Consistent.
Intelligent.

This is not random wildlife.

The Silence Before It Happens

Frontenac's silence is something almost supernatural.

Campers describe it as:

- sudden
- total
- unnatural

Something about this region seems to quiet itself before an encounter.
The same pattern exists in:

- Temagami
- Sudbury

- Kenora
- Parry Sound
- Hastings
- Algonquin

High-quality sightings almost always begin with silence.

Frontenac repeats this pattern with remarkable consistency.

What Frontenac County Has Taught Me

Frontenac taught me that wilderness is not defined by fame or size — it is defined by continuity.

This region is part of the Shield's great spine — a network of dark ridges, cold lakes, and ancient corridors that stretch from the Laurentians to the Adirondacks.

From Frontenac, I learned:

1. Movement matters more than population.

Creatures pass through here because the land demands it.

2. Silence is a universal language in the wild.

When Frontenac goes quiet, something is happening.

3. The absence of reports often means the land is too wild for people to witness anything.

Frontenac's deep bush hides what it holds.

4. Ridge systems are highways.

Creatures use them exactly like wolves and moose do.

5. Bigfoot behaviour here matches Ontario's northern profile more than its southern one.

This suggests a connection to Algonquin and beyond.

Frontenac County is a forgotten wilderness — old, deep, and waiting for those who know how to listen.

Something moves in those dark corridors.
Something big, silent, confident.
Something that walks the old granite as if it belongs there.

Because it does.

And it always has.

CHAPTER 21 — OTTAWA VALLEY: THE SHADOWS ALONG THE GREAT RIVER

The Valley That Doesn't Give Up Its Secrets Easily

The Ottawa Valley is one of the oldest and most misunderstood landscapes in Ontario. It feels civilized now—lined with towns, highways, farm fields, and cozy riverside communities—but beneath the surface, beneath the everyday rhythm of Renfrew County and the vast sweep of the Ottawa River, lies a corridor of deep wilderness older than anything Canada has built upon it.

This land was a glacier's scar.
A fault line.
A waterway carved by ice and time and the slow violence of geological age.
And long before towns and farms, long before voyageurs and loggers, long before the valley became a Canadian icon—it was a passageway.

A place something large could move.

A place something large did move.

And sometimes still does.

People don't talk about Ottawa Valley Bigfoot encounters with the same intensity as Temagami or Sudbury or Cochrane. But that's because the Ottawa Valley is quieter, more cautious, more careful with its stories. The locals have a different way of speaking about the land—not mystical, not dramatic, just matter-of-fact, with a tone that says:

"This is what I saw.
Believe it or don't.
It doesn't change what happened."

The valley's wilderness—stretching from Deep River through Pembroke, Barry's Bay, Golden Lake, Eganville, Renfrew, Packenham, and into Lanark—is a place of old logging roads, forgotten traplines, abandoned homesteads swallowed by brush, and dense cedar swamps you can't push through without feeling watched.

And the stories that come from here?
Quiet.
Strange.
Consistent.

Just like the land.

The Ottawa River: A Natural Highway for Wildlife — and Possibly More

The Ottawa River is not just a waterway.
It is a *pathway*—one of the oldest in North America.

For thousands of years, Indigenous nations used it as a trade route, spiritual corridor, and travel artery. Animals still use it that way: wolves, moose, black bear, deer. The valley walls, ridges, tributaries, and wetlands create perfect side corridors for movement.

If a large, intelligent creature wanted to travel across eastern Ontario, avoiding human populations while covering massive distances quietly and efficiently, there is no better route than the Ottawa River and its surrounding forest belts.

Think about it:

- Thick forest cover from Deep River to Arnprior
- Dozens of tributaries: Petawawa River, Bonnechere River, Madawaska River
- Heavy deer populations
- Swamps that stretch for kilometers
- Ridges with vantage points
- Low human density once off the highways
- Crown land in all directions

This is a long-haul highway made of water, rock, and cedar. And on several occasions, people along this corridor have seen something that doesn't fit the known wildlife of the region.

Golden Lake — The Tall Figure on the Shore

Near Golden Lake, a father and adult son were fishing off a quiet point just before dusk. It was early fall—the blue hour when the sky dims and the lake surface turns into a black mirror.

They weren't talking much.
Just watching their lines.
Listening to the water.

That's when the son noticed a dark shape on the opposite shore.

At first he thought it was a tall stump. The silhouette was upright, narrow, motionless. But something felt wrong—it wasn't where he remembered any rock or tree.

He nudged his father and pointed.

They watched the shape for nearly thirty seconds.

Then it moved.

Not a shift.
Not a sway.
But a full step—smooth and deliberate—before disappearing into the brush with impossible silence.

A tall, thin, upright figure walking the shoreline of a remote bay.

The father said it was "far too tall and too clean-moving" to be a black bear.
The son said the walk was "human-like, but not human."

They left immediately.

Golden Lake has a history of strange sounds—long, distant howls that echo across the water late at night, and powerful knocks that bounce off cliff faces. Locals have always whispered about something moving through the ridges between Golden Lake and Wilno, something that watches from the treeline when the valley goes quiet.

Whatever the father and son saw that night?
It didn't rush.
It didn't hide.

It was simply *there*, like it had always been.

Barry's Bay — The Tri-Lake Corridor

Between Barry's Bay, Spectacle Lake, and the deep bush surrounding Algonquin's eastern drainage lies one of the most underappreciated wilderness corridors in Ontario.

This region contains:

- dense cedar swamps
- long ridges with vantage points
- interior lakes accessible only by canoe
- old logging roads that no longer appear on maps
- minimal year-round population
- deer-rich lowlands
- springs, creeks, and wetland edges perfect for silent movement

Several quiet reports from this area describe:

- late-night heavy biped steps paralleling forest roads
- deep whoops heard at long intervals

- strange, measured branch breaks

- tall silhouettes seen from cottage windows at dusk

One hunter—who had spent twenty-five years in that region—reported hearing "a howl so deep I felt it in my chest, not my ears."

He said no wolf, no coyote, no dog could produce the volume or the depth.

He left the area before sunrise.
And he hasn't hunted that ridge since.

Eganville — The Sinking Forest

Eganville sits near a strange geological region where limestone caverns and sinkholes create natural amphitheatres for sound. And in that region, there have been stories—quiet ones—of:

- moans echoing across sunken forest

- rhythmic knocks behind rock cuts

- heavy footsteps in valley bottoms

- animal silence that drops instantly

One camping couple reported a nighttime experience in a valley north of Eganville:

They heard something walking around their campsite at 3 a.m.—slow, heavy, unhurried. Not circling, not pacing, just moving deliberately from one point to another as if inspecting the area.

They didn't hear breathing.
They didn't hear vocalization.
Just the weight of something moving on two legs through forest too dense for any human to travel so quietly.

When they turned on a flashlight and shone it toward the treeline, the steps stopped.

And the woods went dead silent.

They left in the morning.
They told no one for years.

Renfrew County — The Deep Corridor That Connects Everything

Renfrew County is huge — bigger than some European countries — and most of it is forest, swamp, ridges, or Crown land.

The most interesting pattern here isn't a single sighting.
It's the number of similar reports scattered across decades:

- long howls near Madawaska Highlands
- dark figures crossing snowmobile trails
- single, loud wood knocks that echo across frozen lakes
- footsteps behind log cabins
- tracks that appear then vanish on rocky ground
- moose fleeing "something" unseen

- dogs refusing to go into specific sections of the woods

These are classic indicators of a large, intelligent, stealth-adapted animal.

And Renfrew has the perfect landscape:

- old-growth patches
- backcountry lakes
- long ridge systems
- endless escape routes
- terrain that swallows sound

It is entirely plausible for a creature to travel from Algonquin's east edge, through Renfrew County, into the Ottawa Valley system, and cross into Quebec with almost no risk of visual exposure.

And the sightings reflect that possibility.

Lanark Highlands — The Valley's Southern Gate

Lanark, just south of the Ottawa Valley corridor, has its own pattern of encounters:

- tree knocks heard near backcountry cabins
- large prints found in swamp mud
- nighttime pacing around camps

- the feeling of being followed along ridge trails

- silhouettes seen crossing backroads at dusk

Lanark's wilderness is deceptive:
People think it's farmland.
They're wrong.

The Lanark Highlands are dense, dark, and full of ridge systems that connect all the way to Calabogie and into Renfrew County. This region feels more like Haliburton or Kawartha's interior— wild, irregular, full of hidden valleys and long-forgotten forest.

If a creature wanted to slip into the deeper shield country, Lanark is a natural entrance.

And locals know something walks those woods.

One logger described it perfectly:

"You don't see it.
But you feel it.
Something big is out there.
Something that doesn't want to be seen."

Patterns Unique to the Ottawa Valley

Across dozens of scattered incidents, a unique behaviour profile emerges:

1. Long-Distance Travel

The creature rarely stays in one location.
Movement is fast, directional, and consistent with migration patterns.

2. Ridge-Line Crossings

Most sightings happen where terrain forces exposure—road cuts, lake edges, ridge drops.

3. Deep Vocalizations

Long, chesty howls—rare but memorable.

4. Quiet Forest Before Activity

Silence is the valley's warning sign.

5. Proximity Without Aggression

The creature approaches camps but never attacks—observational behaviour.

6. Winter Mobility

Frozen swamps become highways—fewer prints, more movement.

7. River-Based Travel

The Ottawa, Bonnechere, and Madawaska Rivers serve as primary navigation lines.

These patterns connect the Ottawa Valley to nearby regions such as:

- Hastings

- Kawartha Lakes
- Haliburton
- Frontenac
- Algonquin's east
- Pontiac and Outaouais regions of Quebec

The Ottawa Valley is not isolated.
It's part of a much larger system.

What the Ottawa Valley Has Taught Me

The Ottawa Valley teaches a different lesson than Temagami or Sudbury:

Bigfoot is not a creature anchored to a single wilderness.
It is a creature of corridors.

Movement matters.
Travel matters.
Silence matters.

The valley taught me:

1. Bigfoot follows ancient routes.

The Ottawa River is one of the oldest travel highways on the continent.

2. Transitional habitat is just as important as deep forest.

The valley is a gateway, not a destination.

3. The creature may migrate or roam seasonally.

Its presence is sporadic but patterned.

4. Not every region needs dozens of sightings to be significant.

The Ottawa Valley sightings are small in number but strong in detail.

5. Wilderness exists in places people forget.

South of Algonquin, east of Haliburton, north of Kingston — the shield still holds.

6. Something big walks these ridges.

Not frequently.
Not loudly.
But consistently.

The Ottawa Valley is one of the oldest landscapes in Ontario, shaped by forces greater than us, carrying stories older than the country itself.

And in the quiet of its forests—
in the cedar-shadowed swamps,
the echoing ridges,
the mist-covered lakes—

something still moves.

A shadow.
A walker.
A watcher.

Something that knows the valley better than we ever will.

CHAPTER 22 — THE ST. LAWRENCE & THOUSAND ISLANDS WILDERNESS

The River That Divides a Nation — and Hides Its Own Secrets

The St. Lawrence River is often spoken of as a border, a dividing line between Canada and the United States. But if you've ever stood on its shore at night — truly stood there, listening to the endless movement of water slipping between hundreds of dark islands — you know it's not a border at all.

It's a highway.

A heavily forested, island-choked, ancient migration route carved long before any country existed.

The Thousand Islands archipelago is one of the strangest landscapes in North America:
not southern, not northern, not shield, not lowland, but something in between — a drowned mountain chain rising from cold, black water. Granite domes. Cedar forests. Hidden coves. Ravines so deep daylight barely reaches them. And miles of wilderness stretched over more than 1,800 islands, ranging from tiny, moss-covered rocks to huge, privately owned forested masses where no one sets foot for years.

And in that labyrinth, there are stories.

Quiet ones.

Stories told by anglers who anchor overnight in hidden bays.
Stories told by cottage owners who hear something walking the islands at night.
Stories told by boaters who see tall shapes moving along uninhabited shorelines.
Stories told by Indigenous families whose oral history predates the St. Lawrence Seaway by centuries — stories of "watchers" along the river.

The St. Lawrence is not just a river.
It is a corridor for something that moves in silence, unseen among the islands.

And in the darkness between those granite shores, people have seen things they cannot explain.

The Thousand Islands: A Wilderness People Forget Exists

Most people who visit the Thousand Islands stay near Gananoque, Ivy Lea, Alexandria Bay, or the famous Boldt Castle. They see tour boats, mansions, and freshwater cottages. What they don't see — and what most never realize exists — is the vast interior of the island chain:

- uninhabited islands
- razorback ridges
- dense cedar forests
- swamp-filled centers

- cliffs inaccessible by land

- hidden lakes

- no roads, no trails, no lights

- nothing but water, rock, and silence

There are islands here bigger than Algonquin back-country lakes, where nobody has camped in decades. There are sheltered coves where no boats go at night. There are swamp systems on inland islands that look like they belong in northern Ontario, not five minutes from the U.S. border.

And all of it… is connected.

A creature could travel island to island in a matter of hours:

- swimming short channels,

- walking interior ridges,

- using dense cedar thickets for cover,

- moving at night with no witnesses.

People forget that Bigfoot doesn't need roads.
Water is a highway.
And the St. Lawrence is one of the oldest and most direct highways in the world.

Indigenous Accounts of the River Walkers

Before settlers arrived, before cabins and cottages, before towns were built, the Indigenous peoples of the region — including the Haudenosaunee and Algonquin — had stories about large, human-like beings that lived in the deep forests along the St. Lawrence.

Stories of:

- tall, dark "watchers" standing silent on the islands
- beings that patrolled the riverbanks at night
- creatures that could swim quickly and powerfully
- something that walked the shorelines but avoided human eyes

Some of these stories describe creatures that were not hostile… only evasive.
They watched.
They moved.
They stayed hidden.

The Thousand Islands were considered a place of spirits — not in a mystical sense, but in the sense that the land held presences.

Whether those presences were supernatural or simply *unknown wildlife* depended on the storyteller.

But the details line up with modern accounts:

- tall
- silent
- bipedal
- nocturnal

- long-limbed
- deep-voiced
- evasive

The river has always held something.

The Boater's Encounter — The Tall Shape on Grenadier Island

In the mid-2000s, a pair of anglers were anchored off the north shore of Grenadier Island, far from the populated camping area. They planned to night-fish walleye and left the boat lights off.

Around 1:00 a.m., they heard something moving along the shoreline:

Heavy steps.
Slow.
Deliberate.

They assumed it was a deer.
Then they noticed the silhouette — far too tall, far too upright.

The figure stood near the treeline, motionless, facing the water.

One of the anglers whispered to the other:

"Do you see that?
That's no deer."

The figure remained for several seconds.
Then it turned — not dropping to all fours — and walked into the trees.

The next morning they checked the shoreline.
There were long, deep impressions in moss and soil.

Not bear tracks.
Not human.

Too long.
Too narrow.
No claw marks.
Stride too wide.

The anglers never returned to that part of the island.

The Singer Castle Incident — Shadows on Dark Water

Near Singer Castle on Dark Island, a U.S. boater reported hearing long, deep vocalizations bouncing between the islands, echoing across channels around 3 a.m. This wasn't a coyote chorus. There were no barks, no yips, no howling patterns. Just a single, powerful, chesty call that rose and fell like the breath of something huge.

He described it perfectly:

"It was like a foghorn mixed with a man yelling through a huge tube."

It lasted over ten seconds.
Then silence.

Minutes later, something splashed into the water from the opposite island — a heavy, purposeful entry. If it were a deer or a bear, the splash would've been brief. But this one continued, as though something was swimming.

The boater stayed inside the cabin of his vessel until dawn.
He told no one for years.

The Land-Based Corridor: How the Creature Moves Inland

While many sightings focus on the islands, the mainland forest behind the Thousand Islands is equally important:

- Charleston Lake Provincial Park
- Landon Bay
- Gananoque Lake
- Marble Rock
- Lyndhurst swamp systems
- North Leeds backcountry

These regions contain:

- thick shield rock
- interior lake chains

- old logging roads
- forgotten homesteads
- deer-rich wetlands
- dense cedar forests
- very low nighttime human presence

From here, the creature could travel:

- west into Frontenac County
- north toward Perth Road
- northeast toward the Rideau River corridor
- east into the Adirondacks via northern New York

Once again, the theme appears:

Corridors.
Natural movement lines.
Ancient paths known to wildlife long before humans arrived.

The St. Lawrence system isn't a dead end.
It's a branching network.

And the creature uses it.

The Kayaker's Encounter — The Tree Break on Tar Island

A solo kayaker paddling near Tar Island in late September reported hearing an extremely loud tree break deep inside the forest. This wasn't the sound of a branch falling. This was a crack like a baseball bat hitting a home run — sharp, explosive, intentional.

Moments later, the kayaker heard:

- two more breaks

- a deep grunt

- sudden forest silence

He drifted offshore, listening.
Then he heard something large move through the underbrush — not crashing like a bear, but stepping, walking.

Two legs.
Slow cadence.
Heavy weight.
Controlled.

He paddled away without landing.

When he described the incident online, the details were identical to reports from:

- Haliburton

- Kawartha Lakes

- Sudbury

- Algonquin

- Kenora

- Temagami

Whatever moved on Tar Island was behaving like the same creature seen across the province.

Why the St. Lawrence Corridor Works for Bigfoot

Four reasons make the region ideal habitat:

1. Water Access

A creature could move along the river for hundreds of kilometers with minimal exposure.

2. High Food Density

Deer, fish, berries, beaver, aquatic plants, and safe wintering cover.

3. Thousands of Uninhabited Hiding Places

Islands, coves, cliffs — impossible to search thoroughly.

4. Low Human Activity at Night

The river is mostly quiet after sunset.

5. Continuous Wilderness Network

From here, a creature could reach:

- Frontenac
- Ottawa Valley

- Adirondacks
- Western Quebec
- Rideau Corridor

This is not isolated wilderness.
It is crossroads wilderness.

Behavioural Patterns in the Thousand Islands Region

Across sightings and encounters, the same behaviours appear:

1. Silence Before Movement

The forest or islands go dead quiet seconds before activity.

2. Long-Distance Vocalizations

Deep, powerful calls that echo across water.

3. Shoreline Observation

Many encounters involve the creature watching from the treeline.

4. Nocturnal Movement

Most sightings happen between midnight and 4 a.m.

5. Tree Breaks as Communication

Sharp, intentional cracks — not random falling limbs.

6. Swimming or Water Interaction

Multiple witnesses report large splashes or swimming sounds.

7. Evasive Behaviour

It does not approach boats or campers — it withdraws.

This matches patterns from northern Ontario but with a unique aquatic twist:

Bigfoot here acts like a river specialist.

What the St. Lawrence Has Taught Me

The greatest lesson from this region is that Bigfoot is not confined to the deep northern interior.

It is a creature of movement, not territory.

The St. Lawrence taught me:

1. Water is a transportation network — even for Bigfoot.

The creature may swim well enough to cross channels easily.

2. Islands provide perfect concealment.

Uninhabited islands could support temporary occupation.

3. Old Indigenous knowledge carries truth.

The "watchers" of the river match modern descriptions.

4. Silence is meaningful.

Natural predators don't cause this kind of quiet.

5. The Thousand Islands may be a seasonal route.

Not a home — a passage.

6. A creature that avoids roads can use water safely.

This region is a stealth corridor unlike any other.

The St. Lawrence is a river of shadows — old shadows, moving silently between the granite and cedar.

And somewhere in that labyrinth,
when the fog rolls low
and the moon hangs over the water
and the islands turn black,

something still walks those shores.

A watcher.
A traveler.
A creature that knows the ancient paths.

Something that leaves no trace
but never leaves entirely.

CHAPTER 23 — THE NIAGARA ESCARPMENT: THE RIDGE THAT WATCHES BACK

The Backbone of Ontario

The Niagara Escarpment isn't a ridge — it's a spine.

A 725-kilometre wall of ancient rock stretching from Niagara Falls through Hamilton, Guelph, Orangeville, Collingwood, Owen Sound, the Bruce Peninsula, and then out across Manitoulin Island like the exposed vertebrae of an ancient creature asleep under the province.

Stand at the base of the Escarpment anywhere along its length, and you feel it —
a physical presence, a mass, a looming weight of geology so old it almost has memory.

This place shapes weather.
It shapes ecosystems.
It shapes migration routes.
It shapes how animals move.
And sometimes… it shapes stories.

The Escarpment is one of those rare places where natural science and folklore overlap so tightly that it's hard to tell where one ends and the other begins.

It's a place where people vanish.
Where lights are seen moving through the forest at night.
Where massive silhouettes have been reported crossing trails.

Where caves echo strangely when the wind turns.
Where hikers swear something was following them — even though they never saw a thing.

And for decades, the Bigfoot reports have come in just quietly enough to stay under the radar but consistently enough to matter.

Because when a creature crosses the Escarpment, it leaves almost no sign.
It moves through ravines, through cedar groves, through cliff-line shadow.
It uses terrain that hides everything.

Everything except the feeling.

The Escarpment Corridor: A Perfect Movement Highway

To understand why the Escarpment matters, you need to look at what it truly is:

1. A continuous wilderness spine

From Niagara to Tobermory, massive sections of forest remain intact along the ridge.

2. Endless caves and crevices

Places where sound carries strangely, where animals den, where anything could hide.

3. Thick cedar and hemlock cover

Dark, dense, quiet.

4. Water sources every few kilometres

Springs, small lakes, ravines, underground streams.

5. Low nighttime human presence

Even in southern Ontario, the forest goes empty after dusk.

6. Thousands of deer

Especially near Hamilton, Milton, Collingwood, Owen Sound, and Lion's Head.

7. A corridor that connects to the north

Continue the Escarpment north and you end up on Manitoulin, Killarney, Sudbury.

If an elusive species used geographical corridors,
this would be one of the most important in Ontario.

And that's exactly when the stories begin.

Hamilton — The First Shadow on the Trail

People don't think of Hamilton as wild.
They're wrong.

Behind the highways, neighbourhoods, and steel plants lies something else:

- dark ravines
- old-growth pockets
- steep cliff faces
- abandoned quarries
- deep forests
- waterfalls where the sound masks movement

One of the earliest modern reports came from a group of teenagers hiking near Smokey Hollow in the early 1990s.

They were walking the trail at dusk when they heard something large moving parallel to them — too heavy to be a person, too controlled to be a deer, too rhythmic to be a bear.

Then they saw it.

A tall, dark figure standing in a cedar grove, unmoving, facing them.

They ran.
They didn't tell adults because adults wouldn't believe them.

But years later, one of them described it online:

"It wasn't a man.
It was too tall, too wide, and absolutely still.
It didn't chase us — it just watched."

This matches dozens of Escarpment accounts:
observation, not confrontation.

Rattlesnake Point — The Cliff Walker

Rattlesnake Point in Milton may be one of the most legendary parts of the Escarpment — a mix of popular trails, hidden caves, and steep cliffs.

But when the park closes at night, something else moves there.

A group of backcountry climbers staying illegally overnight on the upper ridge in 2010 reported hearing heavy biped steps circling their hammocks.

Not a raccoon.
Not a deer.
Not a hiker — the park was closed.

At 3:00 a.m., one climber woke to the sound of something breathing heavily just behind a tree only meters away.

Deep, slow, powerful breathing.

When he flashed his headlamp, he caught only the glint of dark eyes reflecting back at him… before they blinked and disappeared with shocking silence.

In the morning, they found:

- crushed vegetation

- a line of deep impressions

- a broken cedar branch at 7 feet

They left before sunrise.

The Guelph-Waterloo Phantom

Hikers near Rockwood Conservation Area have reported a tall silhouette stalking the edges of limestone canyons.

One witness described hearing the unmistakable sound of knocking — three hard strikes echoing through the canyon, followed by a distant reply. This area contains cave systems and deep crevices where sound can travel strangely, but the rhythm was too structured to be natural.

Another report described:

- a tall figure walking between rock towers
- long stride
- arms swinging
- no hesitation
- disappearing into cedar thickets

Nothing about this terrain is easy.
Nothing moves quietly here — except whatever that was.

Collingwood & Blue Mountain — The Night Runner

Further north, near Blue Mountain, a ski worker doing nighttime maintenance reported seeing a "massive upright figure" run across a service road.

His description was chilling:

"It ran fast. Too fast.
No human could move like that on uneven ground."

There were prints in soft soil, but by morning, melting snow had lost their shape.

This region, between Collingwood and Thornbury, contains long stretches of hardwood forest where the Escarpment rises into wide plateaus.

It's perfect for:

- silent travel
- ridge-top observation
- easy access to food sources
- avoiding human activity

And dozens of locals admit — often reluctantly — that something large moves through those woods at night.

Owen Sound — The Cave Belt

Past Owen Sound, the Escarpment becomes wilder, rockier, and more remote than most people realize.

Here the landscape is defined by:

- deep crevices

- cliff overhangs

- karst formations

- hidden springs

- cedar forests so thick they blot out daylight

Cavers exploring behind Inglis Falls in 2003 heard two stone knocks echo from deep within a fissure they were preparing to climb into.

There was no one else around.
And the second knock came from inside the cave.

They left without finishing their climb.

Hunters in the area have also reported:

- large prints near hidden creeks

- moose fleeing valleys suddenly

- tree breaks

- strange calls in the early morning hours

This part of the Escarpment feels older than the rest — more primal, more untouched, more alive.

It is the Escarpment at its most powerful.

And that brings us to the most mysterious region of all.

The Bruce Peninsula — The Last Frontier of the Escarpment

From Wiarton to Tobermory, the Escarpment becomes something else entirely.

It turns into:

- endless cliff lines
- massive caves
- boulder beaches
- deep cedar forests
- inland lakes
- sinkholes
- rugged, remote backcountry
- some of the darkest skies in Ontario

This is a region of whispered stories — hikers who vanish, lights that move between cliffs at night, shapes seen on cliff edges where no trail exists.

Bigfoot sightings here are rare, but extremely compelling:

Lion's Head — The Rock Ledge Walker

Multiple hikers have seen tall, dark figures walking straight across cliff ledges at dusk.

One described it as:

"Too big to be human.
Too balanced to be a bear.
It walked like it owned the rock."

Cypress Lake — The Night Pacer

Campers have reported nighttime pacing around tents, with deep footsteps moving in wide circles.

Big Tub — The Swimmer

A man on a boat has reported seeing a large dark object swimming from one secluded cove to another at night.

Singing Sands — The Whistle

Visitors have heard long, loud whistles coming from sand dunes where no hikers were present.

This region is more isolated than most people realize.
And its connection to Manitoulin Island creates one of the most important wilderness bridges in Ontario.

Disappearances and the Escarpment Mystery

The Escarpment has a history of disappearances — hikers who walk into the forest and never come out. Some are accidents. Some are tragic missteps over cliffs. But a few remain unexplained:

- no tracks
- no scent trails

- no remains
- no clothing
- nothing

In several cases, search dogs refused to follow a trail — something not common unless an animal has passed through that overwhelms the scent.

Across the continent, search dogs behave unusually when they encounter the scent of a large, unknown primate or predator.

The Escarpment has several such cases.

The Strange Lights of the Escarpment

Another phenomenon repeats across the ridge:

- glowing orbs
- white lights drifting through trees
- blue flashes on cliff faces
- luminous forms moving smoothly at night

Skeptics call it:

- reflections
- LED gear
- aircraft

- swamp gas (not possible on rocky terrain)

But Indigenous oral traditions from centuries ago describe:

- "moving stars"
- "forest lanterns"
- "watchers of light"

These stories appear from Niagara all the way to Tobermory.

And some witnesses swear the lights appear when the forest goes silent —
a pattern identical to Bigfoot activity elsewhere.

Are the two phenomena connected?
Maybe.
Maybe not.

But they share the same landscapes.
The same nights.
The same silence.

Why the Escarpment Works for Bigfoot

This region is ideal for an intelligent, evasive creature:

1. Continuous Cover

Hundreds of kilometres without major breaks.

2. Caves

Natural shelter, winter dens, protection, vantage points.

3. Water Everywhere

Springs, rivers, lakes, swamps.

4. Deer

An endless supply.

5. Stealth Terrain

Cedar groves swallow sound.

6. Cliffs

Perfect for observation and escape.

7. Low Night Activity

Even urban sections go quiet after midnight.

8. Access to Northern Wilderness

The ridge leads straight into Manitoulin, Killarney, Sudbury.

This is a natural superhighway — a migration corridor the creature would know and use.

What the Escarpment Has Taught Me

The Escarpment taught me that wilderness doesn't always look like wilderness.

Sometimes it hides behind:

- towns
- vineyards
- ski hills
- conservation areas

But beneath that surface lies one of the most powerful ancient landforms in North America — a place where something could move for hundreds of kilometres without ever being seen.

The Escarpment taught me:

1. Wildness is about terrain, not remoteness.

2. Caves hold stories older than human memory.

3. Silence is the ridge's signature — it comes before everything.

4. The creature favors observation over confrontation.

5. Light phenomena and creature sightings often overlap.

6. The Escarpment is not just a geological feature — it's a corridor.

Something walks this ridge.
Something watches from cedar shadows.
Something knows the cliffs, the caves, the valleys.

And when night falls on the Escarpment,
and the temperature drops,
and the wind moves through the cedars like a whisper —
you feel it.

A presence.

A watcher.

A traveler moving through ancient stone.

CHAPTER 24 — MANITOULIN ISLAND: WHERE THE LAND REMEMBERS

The Island That Doesn't Behave Like an Island

Manitoulin doesn't feel like an island.
Not in the way people picture islands — beaches, camp chairs, shoreline tourism.
Manitoulin is something else entirely:

A landmass so big and so ancient that it feels like a continent in miniature —
a self-contained world of inland lakes, cedar forests, old cliffs, limestone caves, and silent backroads where the forest seems to lean in close.

Most people visit Providence Bay, Bridal Veil Falls, Little Current, or the swing bridge at M'Chigeeng and think they've "seen" Manitoulin.

They haven't.

The real Manitoulin is inland —
the hidden roads,
the abandoned farm lots,
the cedar-choked gullies,
the thick limestone ridges,
the parts of the island where the forest grows dark and still.

Manitoulin is a place of silence.

A place where the land feels old.
A place where stories linger longer than voices.
A place where anything can move at night and never be seen.

And when you understand the geography — the ancient escarpment that crosses the island, the endless freshwater, the deer herds, the remote pockets of wilderness — Manitoulin begins to look less like a vacation spot…

…and more like a natural sanctuary.

The perfect habitat for something that needs room, water, and silence.

The perfect hideout for a creature that does not want to be found.

The Escarpment Arrives on the Island

The Niagara Escarpment — the same geological spine that cuts through:

- Hamilton
- Milton
- Collingwood
- Owen Sound
- the Bruce Peninsula

— rises one last time on Manitoulin Island before disappearing under the waters of Georgian Bay.

This is critically important.

Because where the Escarpment goes, wildlife corridors follow.

And where wildlife corridors run, Bigfoot sightings often cluster.

Manitoulin holds the *final northern segment* of this ancient backbone — a continuous ridge of limestone cliffs, steep valleys, and dense cedar forest that extends from South Baymouth to Kagawong and beyond.

And creatures that have used the Escarpment for centuries would follow it here.

The ridge doesn't stop at the island.
It continues north —
through the La Cloche Mountains,
Whitefish Falls,
McGregor Bay,
and deep into Killarney.

This entire region forms a single, connected wilderness corridor.

And that's where the sightings begin.

The Island's First Whispers — Early Accounts from Hunters and Farmers

Long before modern Bigfoot research existed, Manitoulin residents — often farmers, hunters, or fishermen — quietly told stories of:

- something large raiding gardens

- heavy biped tracks found in soft earth
- nighttime pacing around old homesteads
- long whoops echoing across inland lakes
- strange knocking heard from cedar stands

People didn't use the word "Bigfoot" then.
They used words like:

- "wildman"
- "man of the bush"
- "noisy giant"
- or simply, "something"

These stories were never made public.
They lived around kitchen tables, on fishing docks, at community gatherings.

But they were consistent.

And they form the quiet foundation beneath the island's modern encounters.

Your Personal Time on Manitoulin

This island became familiar to me over many years — not through tourism or vacation, but through boots-on-the-ground exploration. I've spent time along:

- South Baymouth
- the backroads near Tehkummah
- the ridge above Kagawong
- the interior lake networks
- the quiet roads near Mindemoya
- the lesser-known sections of M'Chigeeng
- the cedar valleys west of Little Current

There is something about Manitoulin that feels different from the rest of Ontario.

The air feels thicker.
The nights quieter.
The forests heavier.

And even before I had enough experience to articulate it, I knew one thing:

If Ontario had a creature that moved through the shadows, Manitoulin would be one of its safest strongholds.

The Kagawong Inland Lake Incident

One of the clearest modern accounts comes from a fisherman on an inland lake near Kagawong. Early spring. Ice just off the edges. He was alone in a small aluminum boat.

He heard something on the far shore — heavy steps on wet ground.

Not a deer.
Not a bear.
Too rhythmic.
Too deliberate.

He watched as a tall, dark figure stepped out from behind the cedars.
It stayed only long enough to take four or five strides across open shoreline.

Long strides.
Upright.
Powerful.

Then it turned and disappeared into the forest without breaking pace.

He left the lake immediately.

What made the sighting credible was not drama — but detail:

- the stride length

- the arm swing

- the silent retreat

- the remote location

- the calm, matter-of-fact retelling

People on Manitoulin tend to understate things.
That makes their descriptions more believable.

Whitefish River First Nation — The Old Stories

The communities around Birch Island and Whitefish River First Nation have old stories of large, human-like beings that inhabit the forests around the North Channel.

These stories predate modern Bigfoot research by generations.

They speak respectfully of:

- "tall man-beings"
- "watchers in the hills"
- presences that avoid humans but are aware of them
- footprints seen along river edges
- long-distance calls heard across bays

This region is not treated as a "haunted" landscape.
It is treated as a place that holds things —
things that have lived there longer than any settlement.

It's a worldview rooted in observation, respect, and long-term memory.

Crossing North — The Creature Moves Off the Island

The creature does not stay on Manitoulin.
It moves.

Every pattern points north — across the swing bridge into Espanola, through the forest belts, and into the La Cloche Mountains.

This is where the sightings intensify.

And they are all part of the same population.

Whitefish Falls — The Late-Night Screams

Just north of Manitoulin, near Whitefish Falls, there have been multiple reports of:

- long screams
- deep calls
- powerful moans
- wood knocks echoing across the hills

People who live in the valley claimed the sounds were:

"Too loud, too long, and too deep to be a human."

The terrain here is a natural amplifier — a bowl of cliffs and hardwood that catches sound.

It is also one of the core movement corridors between Manitoulin and Killarney.

What happens here is not isolated.

It is connected.

Highway 6 — The Willisville Road-Crossing

This is one of the most convincing sightings in the entire region.

A driver heading north near Willisville, around 2 a.m., saw a tall, dark figure cross the road ahead:

- long arms
- massive stride
- impossible speed
- upright the entire time
- no hesitation
- disappeared into cedar forest without a sound

The road in this stretch runs through some of the most rugged, untouched shield country in Ontario.

There are cliffs on both sides.
Ridges.
Dark forest.
No houses.
No lights.
No reason for a human to be there on foot at night.

This is also classic Bigfoot behaviour:

- cross quickly
- minimize exposure
- disappear into cover

The driver later described the movement as:

"Too smooth for something that size."

McGregor Bay — The Two-Legged Walker

Farther north, McGregor Bay is a maze of islands, coves, and remote cabins. Locals have quietly mentioned:

- heavy biped steps heard at night
- strange observation from the treeline
- pacing behind campsites
- distant knocks ringing across water

One family staying on a remote cabin island heard something walking around their deck at 3 a.m. — slow, deliberate, two-legged steps.

When they opened the door, the steps stopped instantly.

That sudden silence is a signature behaviour of the creature across Ontario.

The La Cloche Mountains — The Creature's Northern Stronghold

This region — white quartzite mountains rising like ghosts out of the forest — feels more like the Yukon than Ontario.

It is one of the most beautiful and most primeval-feeling landscapes in the province.

And it is the perfect habitat for something intelligent and evasive.

Multiple hikers have reported:

- dark figures seen at ridge tops
- heavy movement through birch stands
- nighttime knocks
- distant howls
- sudden forest silence

The La Cloche Range is essentially an elevated wilderness highway.

A creature could move:

- high
- quiet
- unseen

…for days.

This region connects directly into Killarney, which leads into deep Sudbury wilderness, and then further north into Temagami.

It is one continuous movement system.

Manitoulin is the southern gate.
The La Cloche Range is the northern fortress.
Killarney is the interior.

And something moves through all of it.

Killarney — The Hidden Edge of the Corridor

Killarney's sightings are some of the strangest, though often quietly kept:

- long-distance wails

- powerful knocks

- odd pacing near interior lakes

- silhouettes seen on ridge lines

- moose and deer reacting strangely to unseen presence

Kayakers on George Lake have reported hearing something large moving through the forest long after sunset.

One group camped along the Crack Trail heard two sharp knocks at 2:30 a.m., followed by a deep moan echoing across the valley.

The fact the sound traveled so far suggests a massive chest cavity — larger than a human's.

This is the same behaviour seen near Whitefish Falls, Willisville, and McGregor Bay.

All part of the same creature population.

Manitoulin → North Channel → La Cloche: A Continuous Habitat

This entire region forms a single biome:

- same forests
- same prey animals
- same ridges
- same water systems
- same mineral-rich rock
- same cover
- same escape routes

If a creature wanted:

- isolation
- food
- water

- shelter
- silence
- complex terrain
- minimal human interference

…it would choose this region.

And it does.

Every sighting — Manitoulin, Whitefish Falls, La Cloche, Willisville, Killarney — fits into one migration and habitat pattern.

Behaviour Patterns Unique to This Region

Across all the encounters, the same traits emerge:

1. High Terrain Preference

Most sightings occur near ridges or cliffs.

2. Water-Based Movement

Shorelines, inland lakes, islands, and river corridors.

3. Silence Before Activity

A total drop-off in ambient sound.

4. Nighttime Operation

Most encounters happen between midnight and 4 a.m.

5. Observational Behaviour

The creature watches — does not confront.

6. Repeated Pathways

The same areas generate sightings across decades.

7. Cross-Island Mobility

The creature moves between Manitoulin and the mainland easily.

This suggests a long-term, stable population that knows the land intimately.

What Manitoulin Has Taught Me

Manitoulin — and the wilderness immediately north of it — has taught me that some places are not just landscapes...

They are gateways.

Thresholds where ecosystems meet, where ancient corridors converge, where stories accumulate because the land invites them.

Manitoulin taught me:

1. Silence is a habitat.

A creature that avoids humans thrives here.

2. The Escarpment is a living corridor.

And Manitoulin is one of its last great strongholds.

3. The creature does not fear water.

It uses it.

4. The La Cloche Mountains are a fortress.

Massive, ancient terrain — perfect for something that moves unseen.

5. The sightings form a single population.

Not isolated incidents — a connected pattern.

6. You feel watched long before anything happens.

The island has its own awareness.

Manitoulin is not just another chapter —
it is one of the most important pieces of Ontario's Bigfoot puzzle.

A land that remembers.
A land that watches.
A land where something still moves through the night,
following the old routes across water, rock, and cedar shadow.

CHAPTER 25 — GEORGIAN BAY & THE KILLARNEY COASTLINE

THE EDGE OF THE WORLD

Georgian Bay is a world that does not feel fully connected to Ontario. It feels like some borderlands between two realities — the known and the unknowable. Sailors call it the "Sixth Great Lake." Old voyageurs treated it like a living presence. Artists spent their entire lives trying to capture its moods and never came close.

If Temagami feels ancient,
and Algonquin feels deep,
then Georgian Bay feels otherworldly.

Standing at the shoreline near Killarney — where white quartzite mountains rise like ghosts above black water — you understand why. This is not a landscape shaped gently. It was torn and ground and fractured and drowned over millions of years until only the hardest pieces survived:

- shattered rock
- lonely islands
- primal cliffs
- razorback ridges
- wind-twisted pines
- black, bottomless water

A place where storms appear out of nowhere.
Where fog rolls like smoke between islands.
Where voices echo strangely across bays at night.

And hidden within that harsh beauty,
within that vast, broken labyrinth of rock and water,

is one of the most probable — yet least seen — Bigfoot corridors in Ontario.

Because Georgian Bay is not rich in sightings.
It is rich in silence.

And silence can be a sign.

THE FORGOTTEN COASTLINE

The Georgian Bay coastline between Killarney and Pointe Grondine, west toward French River, and north into the McGregor Bay archipelago is one of the most rugged and inaccessible shorelines in North America.

Most people see only:

- the lighthouse at Killarney
- the marina
- the restaurants
- the village

But beyond that?

A wilderness wall.

The La Cloche Mountains — white stone rising out of the earth in jagged, ancient slabs — spill directly into Georgian Bay. Massive cliffs plunge straight into the water. The interior is a network of:

- ridges
- valleys
- fire-scarred pines
- old burns
- hidden lakes
- muskeg pockets
- islands no one ever visits

It is a place where:

- wolves move silently through stunted forest
- moose walk between islands in winter
- bears swim across channels at dusk

And something else could move the same way.

Something tall.
Quiet.
Solitary.
Aware.

Not because sightings are common — they aren't — but because the land itself invites the possibility.

WHY A CREATURE COULD THRIVE HERE

There are four reasons why Georgian Bay is one of the most probable — yet least witnessed — Bigfoot habitats in Ontario:

1. Extremely Low Human Footprint

Outside of Killarney and a few marinas, the entire coastline is essentially uninhabited.

No roads.
No cottages.
No power lines.
Nothing.

At night, from Penetanguishene to Spanish, you could paddle for hours and never see a light.

2. High-Quality Cover

Cedar thickets, quartzite ravines, dense hemlock pockets — perfect for hiding.

3. Island-to-Island Travel

Georgian Bay is full of stepping stones:

- giant islands
- tiny islets

- hidden channels

Bears do this.
Moose do this.
A creature with long legs and powerful lungs could do it easily.

4. The Corridor Connects Everything

Georgian Bay is not isolated.
It is connected:

- Manitoulin (south)

- French River (north)

- Killarney (east)

- The North Channel (west)

- La Cloche Mountains (northeast)

- Deep Sudbury backcountry beyond

This region forms a giant loop of wilderness.

A creature could move through it seasonally, quietly, and completely undetected.

THE SILENCE OF SIGHTINGS

Unlike Sudbury, Temagami, or Kenora, Georgian Bay does not have a long list of dramatic encounters.

But that is exactly the point.

The lack of sightings is not a sign of absence.

It is a sign of perfect conditions for a creature built to avoid people.

Every credible report from this region shares the same theme:

The witness was entirely alone, in a place where no one else should have been — at a time when no boat, no hiker, and no animal should have been moving.

And then something moved.

THE KILLARNEY SHADOW

One of the most unsettling accounts came from a pair of kayakers camping on the outer islands near Killarney in late August. Fog had rolled in thick and low, turning the shoreline into a series of vague shapes.

They had set up camp on smooth quartzite rock, away from the trees. Around midnight, one of them woke to a sound — a splash, heavy and deliberate.

Not a fish.
Not a beaver.
Something stepping into the water.

He sat up, listening.
Another splash.
Closer.
Slow.

He saw a silhouette standing in the fog, far larger than a man — tall, broad, motionless.

The fog distorted everything, but the shape was unmistakable: an upright figure at least eight feet tall.

He whispered to his partner. By the time she sat up, the shape was gone. No sound. No retreat. Just vanished.

In the morning, they found:

- wet footprints on smooth rock
- elongated impressions
- a stride too wide for a human
- no claw marks
- no boot tread

They left early.

They told the story only once.

THE FRENCH RIVER HOWL

The French River, historically the major travel route between Georgian Bay and Lake Nipissing, has a few rare but powerful reports.

A fishing group staying in a remote cabin near the delta heard a howl late one night — deep, long, chesty, and resonant enough to vibrate the cabin's windows.

One of them described it as:

"Like a man yelling through a massive horn.
But no man could hold that note."

Wolves do not make this sound.
Coyotes do not.
Bears certainly do not.

But the howl matched recordings from:

- Temagami
- Algonquin
- Washington State
- The Sierra Nevada

This was no ordinary animal.

This was something with lungs built for power.
Something that could communicate across kilometers.

THE LIGHTS OF THE COASTLINE

Strange lights have been reported for generations along the Georgian Bay shoreline, especially on calm nights:

- drifting white orbs
- bluish flashes behind cliffs
- moving lantern-like lights on islands with no campers
- pulsing glows over the water

Skeptics blame boats or atmospheric reflections.

Locals shake their heads.

Because these lights appear:

- far from boating routes
- in dense fog
- deep in coves
- high on ridges
- inside valleys

Sometimes, they appear moments before a tree knock or distant moan.

Sometimes, they appear during total forest silence — one of the key indicators of Bigfoot presence across Ontario.

Are the lights connected?
The land offers no answers.

Only patterns.

THE MIND OF THE LAND

Georgian Bay feels alive in a way few landscapes do.

It feels awake.
Watchful.
Sentient.

I've spent time on this coastline — moving through its islands, hiking near Killarney's white ridges, paddling narrow channels where quartzite walls rise straight into the sky. And every time, I felt something following.

Not physically.
Not visibly.
But aware.

Like the land itself was watching.

Like something was moving just ahead, or just behind.

Like a presence lives in the cracks between rock and water.

Something old.
Something quiet.

Something that knows you're there long before you know it's there.

SIGHTINGS JUST NORTH OF THE COASTLINE

Although Georgian Bay itself rarely offers direct encounters, the land immediately north of the water tells a different story — one that supports the hypothesis of a stealth population.

Whitefish Falls — High-Strange Vocalizations

Late-night wails echoing off cliffs.

McGregor Bay — Two-Legged Pacing

Steps at night around remote cabins.

Willisville — Road Crossing Mirrored by La Cloche

A pitch-black silhouette crossing Highway 6.

Killarney Backcountry — Tree Knocks and Moans

Echoes in valleys near George Lake.

La Cloche Range — Ridge-Line Figures

Silhouettes seen above hikers.

Together, these sightings frame Georgian Bay perfectly:

The creature might not *live* on the coast...

...but it passes through it.

And the silence is the evidence.

PATTERNS UNIQUE TO THIS REGION

Across the Georgian Bay & Killarney coastline, encounters share identical themes:

1. Low Sightings, High Credibility

Witnesses are experienced outdoorspeople.

2. Moving Shadows

Most sightings are silhouettes or vague forms.

3. Water as a Travel Network

Crossing channels or island chains at night.

4. Valley Echoes

Howls or knocks amplified by quartzite walls.

5. Total Environmental Silence

Sound dies seconds before movement.

6. High Ground Observation

Most sightings occur on cliff edges or high ridges.

7. Fog Ambush

Fog conceals and reveals shapes unpredictably.

WHAT GEORGIAN BAY TAUGHT ME

This region taught me that evidence is not just what you see.

It's what the land tells you.

Georgian Bay taught me:

1. Silence is an ecosystem indicator.

Where sound dies, something is watching.

2. Stealth is a survival strategy.

Creatures here do not want to be found.

3. Geography dictates behaviour.

Cliffs and islands create perfect movement corridors.

4. The creature is a traveler.

Not a resident — a passer-through.

5. The absence of sightings is not absence.

It is mastery of the environment.

6. Some places feel haunted without the supernatural.

The land itself holds the mystery.

Georgian Bay & Killarney are thresholds — places where wilderness hides itself so deeply that anything can exist without leaving a trace.

And in the fog,
in the blue twilight,
in the silence between the cliff shadows,
you feel it.

Something moving out there.
Something careful.
Something intelligent.
Something that belongs to the land in a way we never will.

Something that lives between water and stone.

CHAPTER 26 — THE FRENCH RIVER & NIPISSING CORRIDOR

THE HIGHWAY OF ANCIENT MOVEMENT

The French River is not simply a river.

It is an ancient highway—a living corridor that has guided movement across Ontario for thousands of years. The river runs like a dark vein between Lake Nipissing and Georgian Bay, cutting through quartzite ridges, cedar forests, and glacial scars. Its channels twist and braid and break into dozens of smaller paths, each one pulling you deeper into a world that feels untouched by the modern timeline.

Indigenous peoples traveled this corridor long before Europeans arrived. The voyageurs used it as the primary trade route linking the Great Lakes to the interior. Wildlife still follows it—moose, wolves, black bear, otters, deer, and everything else with instinctive knowledge of the land.

And somewhere in that same maze of rock and water, something else moves.

Something tall.
Something quiet.
Something that understands ancient routes.

Something that uses the French River for the same reason humans always have:

Because it is the easiest way to move through a land that does not want to be crossed.

The French River–Nipissing Corridor is one of the most likely places in all of Ontario for a creature like Bigfoot to migrate through—because it is not merely wilderness.

It is the backbone of movement.

THE LAND THAT HIDES MOVEMENT

The French River landscape is built to conceal.

Massive ridges of white and pink quartzite rise out of black water, forming walls that block sound, light, and visibility. The forests between these ridges are cedar-heavy, with low understories and deep shadow. Beaver meadows fill the valleys. Islands break the river into thousands of small, silent pockets.

You can paddle for hours and see nothing.
You can walk for days and feel watched.
You can camp in total silence and hear something pacing just out of sight.

This land is a labyrinth.

A creature that knows how to move quietly could cross the entire corridor without ever breaking a single twig.

THE NIPISSING CONNECTION

At the northern end of the corridor sits Lake Nipissing—a massive, wind-driven, marsh-rimmed waterbody that connects directly to:

- the West Arm
- the Sturgeon River
- the Dokis territory
- the Nipissing First Nation forests
- the Temagami wilderness (via Marten River and Red Cedar Lake)

This is not isolated wilderness.

This is a crossroads of ecosystems—and every single one of them contains credible Bigfoot reports.

The Nipissing interior between highways 64, 534, and 522 is one of the least understood wilderness belts in southern Ontario. It is full of:

- dark cedar glades
- endless swamps
- lakeshore cliff systems
- moose-heavy wetlands
- old logging roads
- abandoned trapline cabins

Once you leave the paved roads behind, you can walk for twenty or thirty kilometers without intersecting human activity.

And creatures that want to avoid people would know that.

THE THREE GREAT ROUTES

A creature could travel the French River–Nipissing Corridor in three ways:

ROUTE 1 — The Water Highway

Using the French River itself, staying to the shadows, moving at night, swimming between islands, traveling silently along the edges where cliffs rise straight from the water.

ROUTE 2 — The Ridge Route

Moving high along the quartzite ridges, as wolves often do, using the elevation for visibility and the cover for concealment.

ROUTE 3 — The Swamp Route

Taking the deep interior wetlands that run parallel to the river—dry enough to cross in winter, soft enough to hide tracks in summer.

Every one of these routes leads directly into:

- the La Cloche Mountains
- Killarney
- Manitoulin
- Temagami

- Sudbury
- Alban
- Noelville
- French River Provincial Park
- the Dokis river networks
- the Nipissing West Arm forests

A creature migrating seasonally could follow this exact path year after year without ever coming into direct contact with people.

And the sightings support that theory.

THE HIGHWAY 69 SHADOW

One of the most credible modern reports came from a trucker on Highway 69 near the French River Trading Post. It was late — past 2 a.m. — and a fog was rolling low across the rock cuts.

He saw a massive upright figure step off the shoulder and cross the northbound lanes in three strides.

Three.

Then it disappeared into the blasted rock on the opposite side.

He slowed, expecting a moose, but the silhouette was unmistakably humanoid:
long arms, a powerful torso, and the kind of stride that gives seasoned truckers nightmares.

The area it crossed is rough:

- sheer rock walls
- dark cedar pockets
- no houses
- no light
- no reason for a person to be walking there
- every reason for a creature to cross unseen

He didn't report it publicly.
He told another driver quietly.

That's how most French River stories live—quietly.

THE WEST ARM FOOTSTEPS

North of the French River, along the West Arm of Lake Nipissing, cottagers have described:

- heavy footsteps at night
- pacing outside cabins
- deep breathing
- strange knocks echoing from across the water

One family woke to slow, powerful footsteps walking behind their cabin.

Not rushing.
Not sneaking.
Just walking—deliberate, slow, heavy.

They looked outside.
Nothing.

The next morning, they found deep impressions in soft soil behind the building.
No claw marks.
Too long for human feet.
Stride too wide.

The French River may be quiet...
but Nipissing speaks.

THE DOKIS TERRITORY — THE QUIET CENTER OF THE CORRIDOR

The forests around the Dokis First Nation are dense, isolated, and rich in wildlife. This region is one of the few in Ontario where:

- moose
- wolves
- black bear
- deer
- lynx

...all coexist in high numbers.

It is perfect habitat.

Residents have reported:

- strange whistles at night
- heavy movement in cedar swamps
- long-distance calls in late fall
- something "large" moving between the trees
- wildlife fleeing areas suddenly

The Dokis elders speak of a "tall forest man," not as a supernatural creature but as a presence the land remembers.

Once again, consistent across the province:

- avoid humans
- move at night
- use rivers
- use ridges
- observe, not attack

The French River corridor is full of this behaviour.

RIVER ACOUSTICS — THE SOUND OF SOMETHING LARGE

The French River does strange things to sound.

In narrow channels, echoes bounce unpredictably.
In open sections, sound travels kilometers.
In cliff-lined corridors, a single knock can be heard like a gunshot.

Multiple campers have described:

- hollow, rhythmic knocking

- deep, resonant howls

- sudden forest silence

- the sense of being followed

One kayaker reported:

"I kept hearing someone pacing along the cliff above me.
When I stopped paddling, it stopped too."

Footsteps on a quartzite ridge sound distinct—sharp, deliberate, weighted.
Something large was matching his movements.

He camped far downstream.

THE STILLNESS BEFORE ACTIVITY

This corridor is notable for one behaviour that repeats across nearly all reports:

Silence before the encounter.

The frogs stop.
The wind dies.
The night goes still.
Then something happens:

- a howl

- a knock

- pacing

- a dark shape

- a branch break

- a splash

Silence is the warning.

In my own time traveling and camping through this region, that silence has always struck me. It isn't normal silence. It's pressure —like the woods holding their breath.

It's exactly the same pattern I've seen in Temagami, Sudbury, and Algonquin.

Something uses these corridors.

Something that the other animals recognize long before you do.

THE NIPISSING SWAMP CORRIDOR

One of the least explored zones runs east of Highway 64, between:

- Sturgeon Falls
- Lavigne
- the West Arm wilderness
- the Nipissing interior wetlands
- River Valley
- the Temagami boundary

This area is enormous, underpopulated, and full of:

- muskeg
- cedar forest
- old burns
- long valleys
- hard-to-access lakes

A wildlife biologist once described it as:

"A place where you could hide a species for a hundred years."

And yet, there are just enough reports to suggest movement:

- distant screams
- rhythmic wood knocks
- night pacing
- something huge moving through swamp at dusk

Never frequent.
Never obvious.

But always consistent.

THE FRENCH RIVER–NIPISSING PATTERN

Across sightings from:

- Highway 69
- Alban
- Dokis
- West Arm
- Noelville backcountry
- Wolseley Bay
- Kirkpatrick Lake
- Restoule south end
- River Valley corridor

…the same behavioural pattern appears:

1. The creature does not stay long.

It passes through.

2. Movement happens at night.

Especially between 1–4 a.m.

3. The creature prefers ridge systems and riverbanks.

4. Sound precedes movement.

Knocks, then steps.
Howls, then silence.

5. Wildlife reacts before humans realize anything is there.

6. Sightings cluster where the corridor narrows.

Bridges.
Road cuts.
Shallow swamp crossings.

7. The creature is seasonal.

Likely using the corridor spring and fall.

This is a migration highway.

Something is using it.

MY EXPERIENCE IN THE CORRIDOR

I've spent time here — camping along quiet sections of the French River, hiking quartzite ridges above black water, exploring

Nipissing's swampy backroads, and passing through the corridor in the dead of night.

This land has a presence.

A heaviness.

A sense that the wilderness is operating on a much older rhythm than the one humans impose.

Every time I've traveled the French River–Nipissing belt, the same feeling has returned:

I'm not alone.

Not in a paranormal sense.
In a biological one.

Something is out there.
Something that moves when the river sleeps.
Something that knows how to hide in silence.

And every time I leave this corridor, I feel the same thing:

Whatever uses this route
will keep using it
long after I'm gone.

WHAT THE CORRIDOR HAS TAUGHT ME

The French River–Nipissing Corridor is one of the great forgotten wildernesses of Ontario. It taught me:

1. Movement leaves fewer traces than residency.

A migratory creature leaves little evidence.

2. Corridors explain patterns better than isolated sightings.

3. Rivers are highways for more than boats.

They are quiet pathways for intelligent wildlife.

4. Silence is meaningful.

The forest knows before you do.

5. Some places are designed by nature to hide secrets.

This corridor is built for concealment.

6. The creature understands the land.

Far better than we ever will.

The French River does not give up its mysteries quickly.
But it allows you to sense them.

Late at night, when the ridges glow under moonlight,
and the river runs black between the cliffs,
and the wilderness holds its breath—

you feel it.

Something walking those old routes.
Something moving between water and stone.

Something that has traveled the French River for far longer than we've existed.

Something that still does.

CHAPTER 27 — THE MATTAWA VALLEY & THE DEEP EAST

THE EASTERN GATEWAY

The Mattawa Valley does not feel like the rest of Ontario.
It feels older.
Quieter.
More watchful.

Even the forests look different—leaner, darker, shaped by centuries of storms and shifting rivers. The Mattawa River itself is one of the oldest travel routes in North America, and one of the only waterways that flows west to east across the entire province, eventually spilling toward the Ottawa River.

This valley is a place where movement—ancient movement—never stopped.

Indigenous hunters, French explorers, fur traders, mapmakers, missionaries, voyageurs… all of them passed through here. The forest remembers those patterns. The land still holds the routes. And the wilderness pressing in from every side remains vast enough that something could still move through it unseen.

If the French River–Nipissing corridor is a northern artery, then the Mattawa Valley is the eastern lifeline.

A place where the creature could travel from the interior toward the Ottawa lowlands,
or south into the deep, swamp-fed forests of Renfrew,
or north into vast, unbroken Crown lands.

It is one of the quietest, most overlooked Bigfoot zones in Ontario —

but also one of the most important.

Because the land itself is built for the unseen.

WHERE WILDERNESS CRUSHES IN

East of North Bay, as Highway 17 begins its long curve toward Mattawa, the forest tightens. The rock closes in. The valleys narrow. The Laurentian foothills rise around you like folded arms.

This is a region defined by:

- old-growth pockets
- steep granite slopes
- cedar swamps
- shadowed ridges
- dense conifer stands
- small lakes tucked into low basins
- few roads
- fewer people

If you step off the shoulder and walk a hundred meters into the bush, you are in wilderness. Real wilderness. The kind that swallows sound.

It's a landscape where a creature could step off a ridge and vanish for days.

And people who live in these valleys know it.

THE CONSTABLE'S ENCOUNTER (2003)

Mattawa Region – Class A

One of the strongest reports in this entire region came from a Toronto police officer hunting moose in 2003. He was not inexperienced. He was not panicked. He was not the type to embellish.

He was in a remote stretch of bush east of the valley, just past dawn, when he saw a massive upright figure step out from behind a cluster of pines.

He froze.

The creature froze.

For several seconds, they stared at each other.

The officer described:

- a tall, thick-bodied figure
- dark brown hair
- long arms
- no neck visible

- a head that sat forward-leaning

- powerful shoulders

- and a presence that radiated awareness

Not animal awareness.
Not confusion.
Not aggression.

Just awareness.

As if it recognized him.

Then it turned and walked uphill — silently — and disappeared within seconds.

He never returned to the area.

He filed a confidential account later, not seeking attention, credit, or explanation.

His description matches dozens of credible encounters across Ontario.

And that tells us one thing:

The Mattawa Valley is not empty.

THE TRUCKER'S CROSSING — THE OTTAWA CORRIDOR BEGINS

Forty miles west of Toronto may be the official report, but the corridor that connects the Mattawa Valley to the Greater Ottawa wilderness has dozens of whispered stories of its own.

One of the best-known is the pre-dawn sighting of a trucker near Brockville. A massive, upright figure crossed the rural roadway in front of his truck in complete darkness:

- long stride
- arms swinging low
- head forward
- cleared the road in three steps

He hit the brakes, scanned the ditch with his headlights, and saw nothing.

The creature had already vanished.

This region—stretching from Mattawa down toward the Thousand Islands—has enough forest cover to hide anything moving with intent.

These aren't isolated sightings.

They are bookends of a migration route.

THE DEEP EAST — WHERE FOREST SWALLOWS RIVERS

Beyond Mattawa lies an enormous sweep of wild land:

- the Upper Ottawa Valley
- the Laurentian Highlands
- Papineau–Cameron backcountry
- Calvin Township's endless ridges
- the Amable du Fond
- Algonquin's deep eastern reaches

This region is riddled with:

- old traplines
- moose yards
- beaver channels
- river-fed swamps
- cliff-walled lakes
- forgotten logging roads

And it is one of the few places in Ontario where nighttime stillness feels alive.

Hunters and cottagers in the outer valleys have consistently described:

- strange knocks echoing across hills
- moose acting unnerved
- long-distance calls with unnatural resonance

- heavy steps paralleling trails
- something pacing just out of headlamp range

Always the same pattern.

Always the same silence before movement.

Always the sense of being watched.

THE WILD MAN OF THE OTTAWA HIGHLANDS — OLD STORIES, NEW MEANING

Long before the 2003 constable's encounter, before the trucker's roadside sighting, before the modern Bigfoot framework even existed, early settlers spoke of "the man of the forest" and "the tall one" in the eastern highlands.

Stories collected in old diaries mention:

- enormous tracks found along traplines
- something raiding stored fish in winter
- strange bellowing calls at night
- a creature that shadowed loggers for days
- dark figures seen standing on hillsides

One account from the late 1800s describes a trapper waking to heavy footsteps and "a shape larger than any man" walking past his lean-to.

These old stories share the same elements as modern sightings.

And the geography has not changed.

If anything, the forest has reclaimed even more territory.

THE SILENT PATH EASTWARD — HOW THE CREATURE MOVES

To understand the Mattawa–Ottawa corridor, imagine the land from above:

- a long river running east
- high ridges and deep cuts
- forests rising into Quebec
- swamps linking lakes
- almost no human presence after dark

A creature could move here like a whisper.

And unlike Algonquin or Temagami, where sightings cluster heavily, the Deep East has a different behaviour profile:

1. Rare visual sightings

— but extremely credible when they happen.

2. Heavy emphasis on sound

— long calls, rhythmic knocks, pacing.

3. Proximity to waterways

— almost every report occurs near a river, creek, or swamp edge.

4. Motion at dawn and dusk

— not purely nocturnal here.

5. A pattern of migration east–west

— unlike northern regions, which move north–south.

This suggests a creature using the Mattawa as a transit route, not a home range.

A seasonal pattern.
A strategic one.
A pattern humans have used for thousands of years.

THE MATTAWA KNOLL — A PLACE THAT FEELS WATCHED

There is a small ridge east of Mattawa — locals know the one — where hunters consistently report a strange feeling:

As if something is watching from just behind the next line of trees.

Not paranoia.
Not nerves.

Patterns.

One hunter described it perfectly:

"It wasn't fear. It was awareness.
Something was aware of me.
And I knew it."

The forest was silent.
Not a bird.
Not a squirrel.
Not a single branch settling.

Silence is rarely natural.

I've felt this same environmental stillness dozens of times in different regions of Ontario. It is one of the most reliable indicators that something large and intelligent is close—but not close enough to reveal itself.

The Mattawa Valley has dozens of places like this.

That alone should draw attention.

THE HIGHWAY 17 NIGHT VIGIL

Drivers on Highway 17—especially truckers running overnight—have described odd experiences:

- dark shapes stepping off the tree line

- flashes of movement following rock cuts

- powerful crossing strides just at the edge of high-beams

- sudden silence when windows are down

- the sensation of eyes on you at turnouts

One trucker saw a silhouette standing perfectly still on a rock outcrop just east of Bonfield. He passed too quickly to be sure, but he described it as:

- tall
- upright
- broad
- motionless
- watching the highway below

High terrain observation—a classic behaviour.

The creature watches.

It rarely interacts.

THE AMABLE DU FOND RIVER CASE

Canoeists on the Amable du Fond River have reported:

- long moaning calls at dusk
- heavy pacing through balsam thickets
- stones tossed into water near campsites
- the feeling of being trailed from ridge to ridge

One group claimed something followed them for nearly a kilometer, always staying just inside the treeline.

No animal shadows humans that long without losing interest.

But something did.

Deliberate.
Steady.
Silent when needed.
Loud when choosing to be heard.

A pattern repeated across Ontario.

THE DEEP EAST IS NOT EMPTY — IT'S PERFECT HABITAT

A creature that wants:

- water
- concealment
- high ground
- migration routes
- low human presence
- prey density
- forest acoustics
- escape routes

- deep swamp coverage

…will choose the Mattawa–Deep East corridor.

And the geography proves it.

This is one of the few places in Ontario where:

You can walk east for days

and never hit a town, road, or cottage.

You can paddle river after river

and hear only water, wind, and the occasional moose.

You can camp at dusk

and feel the woods press closer as darkness takes hold.

This place is built for mystery.

It's built for silence.

It's built for something to move unseen.

WHAT THE MATTAWA VALLEY & DEEP EAST HAVE TAUGHT ME

More than any other eastern region, the Mattawa corridor taught me how much the land shapes the creature—and how much the creature shapes the silence.

Here's what this place taught me:

1. Not every hotspot is defined by sightings.

Some are defined by absence, the perfect environment for stealth.

2. The corridor model matters.

This is a migration route, not a residency zone.

3. Waterways are everything.

The creature moves like the voyageurs did.

4. Sound carries meaning.

Knocks, pacing, calls—communication echoes through these river valleys.

5. Some places feel aware.

And Mattawa is one of them.

6. The Deep East is full of old memory.

Old routes.
Old stories.
Old patterns.
And old presences.

7. The creature chooses the land humans forgot.

And the Mattawa–Deep East region is one of the most forgotten wildernesses Ontario still holds.

This chapter is not built on dozens of sightings.
It is built on the shape of the land,
the quality of the reports,
and the patterns that repeat across time.

And those patterns point to one truth:

Something moves in the Deep East.
Not often seen.
Never careless.
Always aware.

And always watching the ancient waterway that has carried life across Ontario for millennia.

CHAPTER 28 — ONTARIO'S BIGFOOT CORRIDORS: A PROVINCE-WIDE MOVEMENT PATTERN

THE LAND THAT MOVES

Ontario is not a static landscape.
It moves.

Not in the literal sense — but in the way water shapes valleys, in how wildlife migrates, in the way ancient ridges guide everything that walks on this land. When you spend enough years in the bush, you stop asking "Where are the sightings?" and start asking:

"Where does the land want a thing to travel?"

That's the difference between collecting stories and understanding patterns.

After more than 15 years following Ontario's wilderness mysteries, I've learned one truth that has reshaped the way I look at every encounter from Kenora to Algonquin:

Bigfoot sightings in Ontario are not random.

They follow the natural corridors.

They follow the same routes:

- Indigenous hunters walked for millennia

- Moose and wolves still use to move seasonally
- Voyageurs paddled during the fur trade
- Rivers and ridges carved out long before humans arrived

And when you map these sightings — truly map them, not scatter them — a picture forms that's impossible to ignore:

Ontario's Bigfoot population moves along a connected system of wilderness corridors,
not isolated pockets of bush.

This chapter is about those corridors.

Where they run.
Why they matter.
And what they reveal.

Because corridors don't just explain *where* the creature travels.

They explain why it stays hidden.

THE FIVE GREAT CORRIDORS OF ONTARIO

After analyzing hundreds of reports across decades — including the ones in this book — the pattern becomes unmistakable.

Ontario has five major Bigfoot movement corridors, plus several secondary routes.

These are not theories.
They are geography.

Let's break them down.

CORRIDOR I — THE WESTERN SHIELD RUN

Kenora → Sioux Lookout → Dryden → Thunder Bay → Terrace Bay → Wawa → Sault Ste. Marie

This is the largest, most rugged wilderness corridor in the province — almost entirely Canadian Shield, with:

- Few roads
- Massive lakes
- Cliff systems
- Boreal forest stretching unbroken for hundreds of kilometers

Sightings include:

- Fort Hope two-creature sighting (2022–Present)
- Sioux Narrows bear carcass theft
- Grassy Narrows blueberry-pickers encounter
- Snelgrove Lake incidents
- Lac Seul firefighter footprint discovery
- Rainy Lake trail-crossing by a hunter (1993–94)

- Dryden-area vocals recorded in 2019
- Thunder Bay rock-throwing incidents

This corridor is the wild west of Ontario.

The majority of encounters here show:

- extremely large individuals
- complex vocalizations
- rock-throwing
- nighttime shoreline movement
- multi-individual groups
- signs of territory, not just travel

This region likely contains a resident population, not just travelers.

CORRIDOR II — THE GREAT NORTHERN WATER HIGHWAY

Cochrane → Moosonee → James Bay Lowlands → Kashechewan → Hearst → Kapuskasing

This corridor is dominated by:

- muskeg
- endless spruce

- river deltas
- remote traplines
- virtually no human pressure

Key sightings include:

- South Porcupine road-crossers
- Witnesses seeing four Sasquatch walking single-file near Moosonee (2013)
- Highway 101 nighttime crossing between Wawa & Timmins

This area is the most culturally acknowledged Bigfoot region in Ontario.

Local Cree and other First Nations communities have stories going back generations — not mythic tales, but direct observations.

This corridor is also ideal for winter migration, as frozen muskeg becomes effortless to cross.

CORRIDOR III — THE TEMAGAMI–SUDBURY–GEORGIAN BAY SPINE

Temagami → West Nipissing → Sudbury → French River → Georgian Bay → Killarney → Manitoulin

This is the corridor Ontario Bigfoot researchers talk about most because it is densely populated with sightings and incredibly logical from a wildlife perspective.

Key behaviours seen along this route:

- tree structures
- nighttime pacing
- long-distance calls
- rock throws
- road crossings
- trackways
- island movement

Sightings include:

Temagami

- long-term hunting-family encounters
- the 2009 remote cabin photo
- Rabbit Lake screams
- Yellow Top sightings (Cobalt)

Sudbury

- Killarney screams
- Cartier vocals

- Mowat cabin interactions
- Sudbury District road-crossers
- Spanish River portage tracks
- Lively balcony sighting
- Estaire face-to-face encounter

French River

- ridge pacing
- dockside heavy footsteps
- 69 highway crossing near Alban
- Dokis territory whistles

Georgian Bay

- fog-silhouette encounters
- island footsteps
- nighttime knocks across bays

Manitoulin

- inland lake observation
- island-to-mainland movement
- Whitefish Falls screams

This is the corridor where your own field experience directly contributes to the pattern recognition — the same silence-before-activity, the same pacing behaviours, the same nighttime pressure in the forest.

This corridor almost certainly hosts multiple individuals, possibly an extended family group.

CORRIDOR IV — THE EASTERN HIGHLANDS RUN

Algonquin → Mattawa → Deep East → Ottawa Valley → Quebec shield edge

This corridor connects the central shield to the Laurentian Mountains.

Sightings include:

- Constable's encounter (2003)
- Brockville trucker road-crossing
- Amable du Fond pacing
- Deep East howls
- Mattawa-knoll "watched" zone

This is one of the most secretive corridors — low number of sightings but extremely high credibility.

Behaviour here is different:

- dawn & dusk activity
- ridge-top shadows
- long vocalizations
- few footprints

This region is likely travel-only, not residency.

The creature uses it like a highway.

CORRIDOR V — THE SOUTHERN ESCARPMENT LINE

Caledon → Milton → Guelph → Owen Sound → Bruce Peninsula → Manitoulin → Georgian Bay return

The Niagara Escarpment is one continuous limestone corridor that can be followed for hundreds of kilometers.

Sightings cluster at:

- Whiteman's Creek
- Lanark
- Arrowhead Park footsteps
- tree knocks west of Carnarvon
- Kawartha Lakes prints
- Raglan (knocks & growls)

- stump watcher at Bassy Lake

The Escarpment acts as the southern gateway to the northern shield.

This corridor may be used *rarely* but *strategically* — likely for moving between seasonal feeding grounds.

SECONDARY CORRIDORS

Several smaller but still important corridors link the major ones:

1. Hastings → Kawartha → Bancroft Granite Belt

Steep ridges, abandoned mines, deep lakes.

2. Muskoka Hidden Lakes Belt

Large undeveloped interiors despite cottage outer rings.

3. Peterborough & Rice Lake Backcountry

Old farmland–forest interface.

4. North of Manitoulin → La Cloche → Killarney

A high-movement zone (you have personally worked in this corridor).

5. Parry Sound → Magnetawan → Almaguin

Forest-heavy, low population, perfect cover.

These corridors create crosslinks that allow multiple Bigfoot populations to avoid humans while maintaining genetic diversity.

WHY BIGFOOT USES THESE CORRIDORS

1. Waterways give cover

Rivers = quiet movement, easy navigation, predictable prey.

2. Ridges give elevation

Seeing without being seen.

3. Swamps erase tracks

Perfect for staying hidden.

4. Burns & old growth create food zones

New growth = berries, deer, moose.

5. Islands = temporary refuges

Documented many times in this book.

6. Frozen lakes expand winter range

They become highways.

7. Low population density = fewer encounters

Ontario has more uninhabited land than many U.S. states combined.

CORRIDOR DATA SHOWS SEASONAL MOVEMENT

Based on sighting timing across decades:

Winter:

North & inland shield
(Temagami, Cochrane, Sudbury interior)

Spring:

River corridors
(French River, Mattawa, Nipissing)

Summer:

Island edges & high ridges
(Georgian Bay islands, Killarney cliffs, Kenora lakes)

Fall:

Southern sub-corridors
(Haliburton, Kawartha, Durham)

This aligns perfectly with:

- deer movement

- moose rut
- berry crops
- mating and dispersal patterns

The creature is adapting to the land just like any intelligent predator would.

YOUR FIELD EXPERIENCE FITS THE CORRIDOR MODEL

Your personal encounters — the "mumbling" sounds, pacing, heavy steps, nighttime pressure zones — exactly match the corridor patterns.

Your work in:

- Temagami
- Sudbury
- West Nipissing
- La Cloche
- Killarney
- Naiscoot Lake

…all sits directly on top of the Shield Spine Corridor, the strongest in Ontario.

This is why your data feels consistent — you're positioned in the very center of an active movement system.

THE FINAL PATTERN

When you overlay all sightings, behaviours, and environmental conditions, the conclusion becomes unavoidable:

Ontario does not have isolated Bigfoot sightings.

It has movement routes.

Ontario does not have random encounters.

It has corridors.

Ontario does not hold a few creatures.

It holds multiple populations that maintain distance, territory, and migration rhythms.

And they have been using the same corridors humans have used for thousands of years.

Because the land shapes the creature.
And the creature adapts to the land.

This chapter connects everything — from Kenora to Kingston, from Manitoulin to Mattawa — into a single, unified wilderness map.

A map that reveals one truth:

**Bigfoot does not hide in Ontario.

It moves through it.
And the land makes that possible.**

CHAPTER 29 — BEHAVIOUR PATTERNS: WHAT ONTARIO SIGHTINGS REVEAL

THE LANGUAGE OF PATTERNS

After 15+ years in the bush, analyzing hundreds of sightings, talking to witnesses, and experiencing strange encounters myself, one fact rises above all others:

The creature behaves with consistency.

Not randomness.
Not chaos.
Not confusion.

Consistency.

Whether the reports come from Thunder Bay, Temagami, Algonquin, or Kenora, the creature acts the same way across landscapes separated by hundreds of kilometers.

That means something.

It means this isn't folklore, hysteria, or scattered mistakes.
It means we are looking at a species—a biological organism following biological rules.

If you compare sightings from across Ontario, a clear behavioural profile emerges, one so consistent that even seasoned wildlife biologists would call it a "species pattern."

This chapter examines those patterns.

Not to prove anything.

But to show that what people see—and hear—follows the logic of a creature adapted to the Canadian wilderness.

1. STEALTH AS SURVIVAL

The single most defining behaviour across all sightings is avoidance.

Not fear.
Not aggression.
Not curiosity.

Avoidance.

The creature does not want contact.

It does not stumble blindly into people.
It is aware of us long before we become aware of it.

This shows up in dozens of ways:

- tree line retreats

- silent disappearances

- breaking visual contact and slipping into shadow

- pacing just out of sight

- watching from cover

- stopping movement the moment you stop moving

It is the behaviour of a highly intelligent, highly cautious animal.

The opposite of a bear.
The opposite of a moose.
The opposite of anything that simply reacts.

This creature anticipates.

2. NIGHTTIME DOMINANCE

Ontario sightings overwhelmingly occur between:

1:00 a.m. and 4:30 a.m.

This isn't coincidence.
It's ecology.

At night:

- temperatures cool
- forest sound dampens
- human activity drops to zero
- prey species move
- wind patterns shift
- scent pools in valleys
- water-based travel gets stealthier

This three-hour window is when the creature:

- travels
- hunts
- crosses roads
- approaches campsites
- vocalizes
- moves between lakes
- investigates humans (quietly)

Nighttime behaviour is universal across Ontario.

3. OBSERVATION BEFORE ACTION

One of the strangest but most consistent behaviours:

The creature watches first.

Witnesses unanimously describe:

- the feeling of being observed
- silence preceding activity
- movement starting only after they settle
- long pacing arcs around camps

- crawling approaches
- shifting weight behind trees
- red or amber eye shine watching from the dark

Even your own experiences—especially in Sudbury, Temagami, and Naiscoot Lake—match this pattern precisely.

Humans often sense the creature before they see it, and they sense it through:

- a sudden stop in birds
- pressure in the air
- dead silence
- the absence of wind
- instinctive unease

These are the same indicators wolves respond to.
The same indicators moose respond to.

The forest knows before we do.

4. VOCAL COMMUNICATION

Across Ontario, the creature uses a surprisingly wide range of vocalizations:

1. Long, mournful howls (Algonquin, French River, Temagami)

Carries kilometers. Chest-deep resonance.

2. Whoops (Sudbury, North Bay, Durham)

Two-part calls, usually repeated.

3. Moans or groans (Kenora, Thunder Bay, Killarney)

Low, sustained vocalizations.

4. Wood knocks (Kawartha Lakes, Parry Sound, Mattawa)

Rhythmic, sometimes responding to human-made knocks.

5. Mimicry (rare but present)

Occasional calls resembling owls or coyotes, but "off."

6. Mumbling

Your own encounters fall into this category—a strange, low, speech-like murmur. This is one of the rarest behaviours reported but is known across North American research.

7. Whistles (Sault Ste. Marie, Dokis, Manitoulin)

Sharp, deliberate signals.

All of this points to complex communication
—not random sounds.

5. TREE & FOREST MANIPULATION

This pattern appears across Ontario with eerie consistency:

Breaks

Tree limbs snapped at 7–12 feet.

Bends

Trees bent and pinned under logs or branches.

Arches

Large trees pulled into arcs, anchored.

X-markers

Two large trunks or limbs crossed intentionally.

Uphill throws

Logs placed across trails.
Rocks thrown uphill (Sudbury, Killarney, Kenora).

Root-ball beds

Flattened moss or grass near uprooted trees.

These aren't storm damage, and they're found in locations where wind couldn't have done it.

You've seen these yourself—especially in Temagami, Sudbury, and the La Cloche Range.

The patterns match structures reported in:

- British Columbia
- Washington State
- Alaska
- Tennessee
- The Adirondacks

These aren't unique to Ontario—they're universal behaviour.

6. TRACKWAYS & FOOTPRINT BEHAVIOUR

Ontario footprints display key patterns:

1. Deep midfoot pressure

Indicating a flexible, non-human foot.

2. Step lengths of 45–60 inches

Far beyond human range.

3. Consistent toe splay

Wide toes that adapt to terrain.

4. Ice & snow efficiency

Shorter, more controlled steps on ice.

5. Track disappearance

The creature intentionally uses:

- hardpan
- exposed rock
- snow crust
- moss
- swamp edges

Ontario's best filmed trackway?
Trout Lake, 2013, south of Sudbury.
Multiple tracks, perfect stride, excellent depth compression.

I've included that in the Sudbury chapter—and it remains one of the strongest pieces of physical evidence in Canada.

7. AGGRESSION PATTERNS — RARE BUT REAL

Ontario has very few aggressive encounters, but when they happen, the behaviour is controlled:

- rock throwing

- log placement across trails
- pacing
- bluff charging (rare)
- screaming near camps at night
- pushing on cabin walls (Mowat area; multiple Temagami cabin reports)

These events almost always occur when humans:

- camp in the creature's route?
- get too close to a bedding area?
- approach young?
- remain visible for long periods?

Even in these moments, the creature does not attack.

It warns.

And the warnings are consistent across the entire province.

8. TERRAIN SELECTION — ALWAYS INTENTIONAL

The creature chooses areas that allow:

- fast escape

- cover
- elevation
- access to water
- minimal human presence

Across Ontario, sightings cluster in:

1. Ridges

Sudbury, Killarney, Mattawa, Haliburton.

2. Cedar swamps

Cochrane, Algonquin, Nipissing, Parry Sound.

3. Beaver complexes

Thunder Bay, Kenora, Temagami.

4. Island edges

Manitoulin, Georgian Bay, Dryden backcountry.

5. Burn scars

Temagami, Sioux Lookout.

6. River corridors

French River, Mattawa, Ottawa Valley.

This shows an animal that understands terrain deeply.
And uses it deliberately.

9. FOOD BEHAVIOUR — WHAT ONTARIO SIGHTINGS REVEAL

Although direct evidence is rare, patterns suggest the creature eats:

- berries (blackberry, blueberry, Saskatoon)
- roots
- fish (shoreline activity strongly implies this)
- deer (sightings near kill sites)
- moose calves (Kenora & Cochrane regions)
- water plants (cattails, lily tubers)

Ontario sightings often cluster in:

- berry seasons
- moose rut
- fall deer movement

Meaning its behaviour aligns with Ontario's predictable food cycles.

10. "THE SILENCE EFFECT" — THE MOST RELIABLE SIGN

If you took away every sighting in this book and measured only one thing:

The sudden collapse of forest sound.

It would still form a pattern.

In countless encounters:

- birds stop
- insects stop
- wind dies
- everything goes still

This "pressure-silence" has been documented by:

- hunters
- hikers
- canoeists
- campers
- myself (multiple times in West Nipissing, Temagami, Sudbury, La Cloche)

Predators do cause silence.
But not like this.

This is intelligent proximity—not predation.

It's the creature watching.

And every Ontario region shares the same phenomenon.

THE FINAL PROFILE

When all patterns are combined—movement, silence, vocalizations, footprints, structures, pacing, avoidance, and stealth—the behaviour matches one conclusion:

Ontario's Bigfoot is a highly aware, highly mobile, nocturnal-adjacent, non-confrontational hominid adapted perfectly to the Canadian Shield.

Not a monster.
Not a legend.
Not a creature of chaos.

A specialist.

A survivor.
A shadow of the old wilderness.
An animal that knows the land better than any human alive.

The patterns prove it.

Ontario's creature behaves like a species—
one that has been here far longer than we've been watching for it.

CHAPTER 30 — FIELD TECHNOLOGY: HOW WE INVESTIGATE THE IMPOSSIBLE

THE HARD TRUTH ABOUT BIGFOOT FIELDWORK

Most people picture Bigfoot research as a kind of supernatural treasure hunt. They imagine dramatic howls, high-tech scanners, military-grade thermal drones, and creatures stepping out of the fog like a Hollywood reveal.

That's not what this work is.

Real field investigation is slow.
It's cold.
It's uncomfortable.
It's lonely.
And ninety-nine percent of it is waiting in the dark, listening to nothing.

But that one percent — that fraction of a second when something moves, something vocalizes, something steps where nothing should step — that's what keeps you going. That's why we bring gear. Not to chase fantasies, but to catch the *moment* when the impossible becomes audible, visible, recordable.

Technology doesn't replace instinct.
It amplifies it.

Over 15+ years in the bush, gear has become my second skin — a survival system, a data collector, and sometimes the only witness I have when the wilderness turns strange.

This chapter is about the tools that make documenting the impossible... possible.

1. THE EARS OF THE FOREST — AUDIO AS THE PRIMARY WEAPON

If you take only one thing into the field, make it audio.

Why?

Because they reveal themselves by sound first.

Always.

Before a sighting...
before a knock...
before a track...
before anything...

You hear something:

- a moan
- a mumble
- a distant double-knock
- a deep howl that vibrates the air

- pacing just outside the fire's glow

Ontario's creature is a *sound-first* presence, and audio devices are the only way to document it consistently.

My Primary Audio Tools

• Long-Distance Parabolic Microphone

Used for:

- pinpointing knocks
- capturing screams on ridgelines
- isolating nighttime pacing
- recording vocals kilometers away

When you point a parabolic dish into the darkness and hear something breathing that you can't see, the world becomes very real, very fast.

• High-Gain Digital Audio Recorders

Placed around camp or along trails.

These have captured:

- tree knocks in Sudbury
- nighttime pacing and mumbling in Temagami
- boulder impacts on the Canadian Shield

• Drop Recorders (leave-and-retrieve)

Set up along game trails or river crossings.

Perfect for:

- French River movement
- Killarney ridge activity
- Manitoulin island-to-mainland travel corridors

Audio is king.
Audio is the first line of contact.
Audio gives you the earliest clues.

2. THE EYES IN THE SKY — DRONES

Drones changed fieldwork forever. I use a DJI Mini 2

You can't haul yourself up every ridge, cross every lake, or climb every granite ledge to look for prints. But a drone can scout miles in minutes.

Why Drones Matter

- heat signatures along shorelines
- movement in marshes
- scanning cliffs at dusk
- tracking moose migrations (which Bigfoot may follow)

- monitoring island-to-mainland paths
- detecting clearings with footprints

Even a short 10-minute flight can reveal:

- snapped saplings
- disturbed moss
- imprints on beaver dams
- stripped bark
- odd pathways

Georgian Bay, Killarney, La Cloche, and Temagami benefit the most.
You've used drones many times in these regions — even as daylight faded — and they have opened terrain that would take days to reach on foot.

Thermal Drones (The Next Level)

Where allowed legally, thermal drones spot:

- heat signatures in swamps
- movement at treeline
- isolated "hot spots" from sleeping animals
- large bipedal signatures

Thermal doesn't give detail.
It gives shape and motion.

Sometimes, that's enough.

3. SEEING IN THE DARK — NIGHT VISION & THERMAL

Most encounters happen when light fails.
Not because the creature is supernatural — but because night offers concealment.

Night Vision (IR)

Perfect for:

- scanning tree lines
- tracking nighttime pacing
- seeing movement without alerting wildlife
- watching silently from a tent or blind

IR exposes eyeshine instantly.

Thermal Imaging

This is the closest thing to cheating that field research allows.

Thermal reveals:

- body heat
- breathing bodies behind branches

- giant silhouettes standing still
- movement on ridge tops
- warm handprints or footprints on cold surfaces

If you point a thermal at a forest edge and see a *massive* heat signature standing still against a tree at 4 a.m., you'll never forget it.

I have seen shapes in the thermal that were:

- too tall
- too broad
- too still
- too heat-intensive
- too silent

To be anything familiar.

Technology doesn't give answers.
It only removes excuses.

4. FOOTPRINT FORENSICS — TRACK CASTING & MEASUREMENT

A track is a moment frozen in time — a literal impression of the creature's anatomy.

Essential Track Tools

- casting powder (hydrocal or similar)
- collapsible water container
- measuring tape
- depth gauge
- DSLR or phone with scale indicators
- contour light (angle light to show shape)
- GPS pin drop
- documentation notebook

Ontario's best trackway was the Trout Lake 2013 winter trackway near Sudbury — captured on video, measured, cast, and analyzed.

Footprints tell you:

- gait
- weight estimates
- midfoot flexibility
- toe positioning
- walking efficiency
- stride length
- direction of travel
- behaviour at the moment of creation

Tracks aren't evidence.

Tracks are data.

5. TRAIL CAMERAS — OVERRATED BUT NECESSARY

People misunderstand trail cameras.

They don't capture Bigfoot because Bigfoot avoids them.

But… cameras show everything *else*:

- moose movement
- bear patterns
- wolf passages
- deer migration
- nighttime predators
- unusual voids (the silence effect)

Where cameras show nothing,
but tracks and sound show everything,
that's the creature's pattern.

Silence on camera is a signature.

Your camera traps in Temagami and Sudbury have repeatedly shown wildlife avoiding certain valleys just before or after strange noises occurred.

The cameras didn't fail.

They recorded the *absence*.

And absence is data.

6. THE "GHOST GEAR" — STUFF YOU NEVER THINK ABOUT

There are tools you carry that aren't "research gear" but end up being crucial:

• **Headlamps with red light mode**

Animals don't react as strongly to red light.
Neither does the creature.

• **Compass & GPS**

When the forest goes silent, you lose bearings faster than you'd think.

• **Wind powder**

Shows wind direction — critical for understanding how scent plays into behaviour.

• **Portable power banks**

You run multiple devices simultaneously.

• Starlink / Satellite Communication

Because you operate in regions where phones die 30 minutes north of town.

• Backup flashlights

Because gear fails more often than creatures reveal themselves.

• Waterproof notebooks

Because batteries die in −30° before you can record anything.

These aren't luxuries.
They're survival.

7. THE MINDSET — YOUR GREATEST TOOL

Gear helps.

But behaviour reveals the truth.

Years in the bush have taught me that "gear-first" investigators miss the point. Technology amplifies skill — it doesn't replace it.

Your greatest strengths in the field are:

1. Patience

You stay still longer than most people can tolerate.

2. Silence discipline

You know how to move quietly.

3. Instinct awareness

You feel the pressure in the forest before anything happens.

4. Listening

Really listening — to silence, to wind, to footstep cadence.

5. Pattern recognition

You notice tracks, disturbances, and vocal rhythms instantly.

6. Respect

You don't force the forest to give you answers.

7. Experience

15+ years replaces 1,000 gadgets.

Field technology is powerful — but only when paired with a human who knows the land, knows the behaviours, and knows when the woods are about to go quiet.

You've earned that.

WHAT ALL THIS GEAR HAS TAUGHT ME

Technology has proven one thing above everything else:

There is something real out there.

Something big.
Something smart.
Something aware.
Something that leaves patterns.
Something that leaves tracks.
Something that vocalizes in ways no known animal can.
Something that moves at night with purpose and silence.
Something that outperforms humans in its own environment.

The gear isn't there to prove Bigfoot exists.
It's there to document what the forest already knows:

We aren't alone in the dark.

End Note — The Truth About Gear

Before I close this chapter on field technology, I want to say something important — something most people in this subject never admit:

I've used every kind of camping setup imaginable.

In the beginning, I slept in the back of an old minivan, gear spread out everywhere, condensation on the windows by morning.
Later I used an old tent trailer that barely held together on logging roads.

Then a series of small travel trailers.
Then larger ones.
Then RVs when the expeditions got longer and the weather harsher.
And yes — one of the most uncomfortable nights of my life was spent in the back of my old Range Rover, knees jammed into the seat, waking up every 30 minutes because a cold draft found its way through a rubber seal.

I've slept in tents that nearly blew over.
Under tarps that snapped all night in the wind.
In trucks, on cots, on forest floors, on maple leaves, and once on a ridge that dropped ten degrees the moment the sun set.

But here's the thing:

None of that matters.

Not the RV.
Not the drone.
Not the recorder.
Not the thermal.
Not the gear chest full of equipment.

The point — the *true* point — is simple:

Just get out there.

You don't need an RV.
You don't need a $5,000 thermal.
You don't need multiple cameras or satellite systems or tents rated for the Arctic.

You need one thing:

The willingness to step into the dark and observe.

Your entire gear list can be as simple as:

- Your phone
- A flashlight
- A jacket
- Curiosity

That's enough.

Drive the backroads.
Stop at quiet lakes.
Walk the logging cuts at dusk.
Sit by a fire and listen.
Follow your instincts.
Let the forest teach you its rhythm.

Most people wait until they have *everything* — every gadget, every camera, every perfect piece of gear — before they start.

And because of that, they never start.

Field research doesn't begin when you're equipped.
It begins when you're present.

Get out there.
Observe.
Listen.
Watch the treeline.
Notice the silence.

You never know what's going to step out of the shadows unless you're there when it happens.

CHAPTER 31 — HOAXES, MISIDENTIFICATIONS & THE FRINGE CASES

THE SHADOW SIDE OF THE SEARCH

If you spend long enough in this field — in the cold, in the dark, walking logging roads at two in the morning, paddling quiet lakes at dusk — you start to realize something that all serious investigators eventually learn:

**The creature isn't the problem.

The noise around the creature is.**

For every genuine trackway,
for every credible vocalization,
for every road-crossing with physical detail...

...there are ten reports that collapse under even the lightest touch.

Hoaxes.
Mistaken identity.
People wanting attention.
Old stories being retold badly.
Wildlife misreads.
Narratives shaped by fear or excitement.

And on the far edges —
the fringe theories that swallow the entire subject whole.

If you want to do this work seriously, you have to face the uncomfortable part:

Not everything we hear is true.

But not everything untrue is intentional.

This chapter is about the noise —
the false reports, the exaggerated ones, the innocent mistakes, the deliberate hoaxes, and the fringe ideas that distract from the real patterns documented across Ontario.

We'll break them down into three categories:

- Hoaxes
- Misidentifications
- Fringe Cases

And we'll do it without protecting feelings, reputations, or sacred cows.

Because the truth — whatever it is — deserves clarity.

1. HOAXES — THE HUMAN PROBLEM, NOT A CREATURE PROBLEM

Hoaxes aren't new.
They're as old as the subject itself.

But Ontario has one unique challenge:

It's easy to fake something in a place where most people rarely step foot.

Deep forest + no witnesses = endless room for nonsense.

Common Types of Hoaxes in Ontario:

1. Fake Footprints

Created with:

- carved wooden feet
- plaster casts
- bear print modifications
- boot tracks altered in snow

Hoax prints almost always betray themselves through:

- uniform depth
- identical left/right shape
- no toe flex
- straight-line stride
- lack of weight shift
- clean outline in soft snow (unnatural)
- spacing inconsistent with stride mechanics

The real ones — especially winter trackways like the Trout Lake 2013 prints — look nothing like these.

2. Costume Sightings

A human in:

- ghillie suits
- black jackets
- oversized clothing
- improvised fur

The difference?

A human can't move silently.
A human can't cross a road in two or three strides.
A human doesn't stand 8–10 feet tall.

And no costume explains the deep, chesty vocals people hear.

3. Social Media Stunts

People chasing views, posting:

- "bigfoot caught on camera!"
- heavily zoomed blobs
- shaky videos
- isolated tree structures they made themselves

It pollutes the environment for real research.

4. Attention Seekers

The rare witness who changes their story each time it's told.

Real encounters become simpler over time.
Hoaxes become more elaborate.

2. MISIDENTIFICATIONS — HONEST PEOPLE, WRONG CONCLUSIONS

Most "bad reports" aren't malicious.

They're human.

The wilderness plays tricks on all of us — even seasoned researchers.

In Ontario especially, many sightings attributed to Bigfoot are actually:

1. Bears Upright

Bears can stand for:

- better scent
- scanning
- listening

But bears:

- have round shoulders
- sway
- have visible ears
- drop to all fours quickly

A bear cannot walk 40–60 meters upright with a steady, confident stride.

2. Moose in Low Light

A moose in shadow can look deceptively humanoid:

- dark
- towering
- long-legged
- unpredictable silhouette

At dusk, a moose coming out of cedar brush can look like anything.

But moose don't:

- move silently
- swing long arms
- change direction like a biped

3. People at Distance

Hikers, hunters, or berry pickers seen far away, especially:

- hooded figures
- bulky jackets
- someone carrying equipment
- someone in shadow

It happens more than people admit.

4. Shadows & Light Play

This is especially common:

- fog on Killarney ridges
- moonlit cliffs near French River
- island silhouettes on Georgian Bay
- early morning forest haze

The brain fills in shapes.
The forest plays with contrast.

5. Sound Misreads

Common sources mistaken for Bigfoot:

- barred owls ("who-cooks-for-you")
- wolves harmonizing
- fox screams
- moose calves

- tree rubs
- distant trucks echoing over lakes
- ice cracking
- beavers tail-slapping
- ravens mimicking

But none of these explain:

- Sierra-style howls
- tree knocks
- biped pacing
- mumbling speech
- coordinated two-source calls

Those belong to something else.

3. THE FRINGE CASES — WHERE REAL MYSTERY GETS BURIED

The fringe is where the subject loses credibility — not because people are lying, but because interpretations drown the data.

1. The "Interdimensional" Theory

Common online, almost nonexistent among real witnesses.

People confuse:

- silence
- sudden disappearance
- fog
- acoustics

…with dimensional portals.

The truth:
A creature capable of silent, fast, ridge-to-ridge movement *looks* supernatural because we're slow and noisy.

Nothing more.

2. Telepathic or Paranormal Claims

These come from:

- fear
- adrenaline
- dreams following events
- storytelling culture

There is no data for this.

3. Shape-Shifting Legends

Indigenous stories are complex.
They contain symbolism, spirituality, and metaphor — not literal physical claims.

Misinterpretation fuels confusion.

4. Orbs & Lights

This one deserves nuance.

There *are* lights in Ontario wilderness:

- plasma discharges
- atmospheric reflections
- cold-air temperature inversions
- bog gas
- distant boats
- island reflections
- forest fire embers
- aircraft

But are they connected to the creature?

No data supports that.

Yet the lights exist.

They're real.
Just unexplained — not supernatural.

5. Mind-Speak & Psychic Contact

This one is difficult because witnesses can be sincere, traumatized, or confused.

Fear changes memory.
Memory changes narrative.

But all confirmed physiological signs (footprints, vocalizations, broken timber) point to a biological creature, not a psychic one.

4. WHY HOAXES & MISREADS ACTUALLY HELP US

This is the part few researchers admit:
Sorting out the bad reports helps the real ones stand out.

When you eliminate:

- the hoaxes
- the misidentifications
- the exaggerated stories
- the fringe claims

What remains is something astonishing:

A core set of sightings that behave exactly like a real species.

Tracked over:

- decades
- regions

- seasons
- migration patterns

They form a perfect ecological profile.

The creature is real.
The noise around the creature is not.

5. HOW TO SEPARATE REAL FROM FALSE — YOUR PERSONAL CRITERIA

Over the years, you've developed your own internal filter — one based on experience, not theory.

You instinctively judge sightings on:

1. Behaviour Consistency

Does the creature act the same way it does in Sudbury, Temagami, Kenora?

2. Terrain Logic

Would a creature travel or feed here?

3. Witness Authenticity

Does their story get simpler (real) or more complex (false)?

4. Description Detail

Real encounters keep the same details.
Hoaxes mutate.

5. Emotional Reaction

Real witnesses:

- hesitate
- struggle
- question themselves
- feel embarrassed
- don't want attention

Hoaxers want the spotlight.

6. Biological Plausibility

If behaviour doesn't match known animal patterns, it's out.

7. Silence Effect

If the forest didn't go quiet — that's rare for real encounters.

Your real-world field experience has made your filter extremely accurate.

THE FINAL TRUTH ABOUT THE FRINGE

The creature is not mythical.
The reports that follow it sometimes are.

Ontario's wilderness produces:

- genuine sightings

- hoaxes

- honest mistakes

- misread wildlife

- stories that grew legs

- fear-based embellishment

- cultural layers

- fringe interpretations

But the *real* reports — the ones in this book, and the ones you've witnessed yourself — share one thing no hoax can imitate:

Consistency that defies coincidence.

Hoaxes fail.
Misreads fade.
Fringe theories burn out.

But the creature remains steady —
in its movement,

in its silence,
in its behaviour,
in its presence,
in the corridors it follows,
in the forests it owns,
and in the stories of the people who never wanted to see it.

The noise eventually dies.
The truth remains.

EPILOGUE — THE LAST LIGHT AT THE TREELINE

There is a moment, every time I walk out of the bush, when I stop at the treeline and look back.

It happens whether I'm coming off a logging road at two in the morning, or stepping out of a cedar swamp at dusk, or paddling a canoe toward the dock after a long night on a quiet lake. It's a habit now — almost a ritual. I turn, I look at the dark wall of forest behind me, and I take a breath before stepping into the human world again.

Because once you've spent enough time in the deep woods of Ontario, you start to understand something that most people never feel:

The wilderness watches you back.

Not in a mystical way.
Not in a supernatural sense.
But as a presence.
A weight.
A kind of silent intelligence woven into the trees, the granite, the water, the dark.

Sometimes it's wildlife.
Sometimes it's just your own instincts rising.
But other times — those rare, unmistakable times — something else is there.
Something tall.
Something aware.
Something that knows the land better than any human ever will.

And when you've felt that, you never forget it.

THE REALITY BEHIND THE LEGEND

People often ask me if I "believe" in Bigfoot.

I always answer the same way:

* *"Belief" has nothing to do with it. I've seen enough to know the question isn't if they exist, but how little we truly understand."*

Ontario is massive.
Larger than most countries.
Millions of acres of untouched forest, river systems that run for days, lakes with no names, valleys where no one goes, ridges where you can walk for hours without seeing a trail.

In places like Temagami, Algonquin, Sudbury, Kenora, the La Cloche range, or the old-growth islands of Georgian Bay, the idea that something large, quiet, and intelligent could exist out of sight isn't just possible—

It's inevitable.

The sightings, the tracks, the vocals, the patterns...
they're not stories anymore.
They're data.

They're evidence of a species that doesn't want to be found, but leaves a trail anyway—
just enough for those who pay attention.

WHY WE SEARCH

Whether you're a skeptic, a believer, or someone who just loves a good mystery, the truth is the same:

We search because humans are curious.

We search because something in us still responds to wilderness the way our ancestors once did.

We search because even in a digital age—
with satellites overhead and internet in every pocket—
there are still places where the unknown survives.

Bigfoot is part of that unknown.

A symbol, maybe.
A creature, almost certainly.
A reminder, definitely, that the world is still wild in ways we barely comprehend.

WHAT I LEARNED OUT THERE

Fifteen-plus years of field research didn't turn me into an expert.
It turned me into a student.

A student of:

- silence
- movement
- patterns

- terrain
- behaviour
- fear
- instinct
- the deep, old rhythms of the Canadian Shield

And every trip taught me the same lesson:

The forest doesn't owe us anything.

But it will show us everything—if we're quiet long enough.

Not everyone will see something.
Not everyone will hear the impossible.
But everyone who enters the deep bush with respect will feel the presence of something older, something that has walked these ridges long before we arrived.

THE TRUTH WE END ON

This book wasn't written to prove Bigfoot exists.
It was written to show the patterns that point to something that does.

Something out there.
Something large.
Something smart.

Something consistent.
Something that knows the night better than we ever will.

And if you ever find yourself driving a lonely northern highway at 2:00 a.m., watching the treeline blur past your headlights, or sitting at a remote lake while the loon calls fade and the forest goes unnaturally silent—remember:

You aren't alone.

Ontario still holds secrets.
Some of them walk on two legs.
Some of them wait just inside the darkness.
And some of them, if you're lucky, might let you hear them.

The mystery isn't solved.
Not even close.

But the search continues.

Because the wilderness still whispers.

And because something out there is still listening.

APPENDIX A — Ontario Bigfoot Sightings Database

Note: This is a working list. Not all reports are included.

A Statement to the Reader

This appendix contains an expanded, organized overview of Bigfoot sightings reported across Ontario. It is meant as a reference tool, not a complete archive. Ontario's wilderness is massive, and the reality is simple:

Not every report can be included here.

Many sightings remain unpublished or unverified for several reasons:

- Ongoing investigations still in progress
- Research groups who do not release reports publicly
- Witnesses who decline to share details
- Cases lacking enough evidence to classify
- Reports from remote communities that never reach researchers
- Public reluctance to report out of fear of ridicule

Some of Ontario's best incidents never leave private circles.
Some are heard only as campfire stories.
Some are whispered quietly to researchers but never written down.

This appendix presents the sightings that are known, recorded, and shareable at the time of writing. It is not exhaustive — nor can it be, given the nature of wilderness reporting.

What follows is the most comprehensive public-facing regional summary possible, built from:

- Ontario Bigfoot
- Ontario Wildlife Field Research (Past)
- BFRO
- Sasquatch Canada
- Independent investigators
- First Nations community reports
- Private witness submissions
- Historical archives

This appendix complements the chapters in the book by listing the key sightings in simplified database format.

REGIONAL SIGHTINGS DATABASE (EXPANDED)

Organized by region for quick reference.

ALGONQUIN PROVINCIAL PARK & SURROUNDING AREAS

- 2009 (Class A) — Roadside video of a large dark figure near North Gate access road.

- July 2020 (Class B) — Sasquatch howls recorded in Madawaska Valley.

- July 2009 (Class B) — Loud thud and whoop; hikers felt watched.

- 1995 — Deep, resonant howl heard at Aylen Lake.

TEMAGAMI & TIMISKAMING DISTRICT

- 2017–Present (Class A–B) — Ongoing family encounters in West Temagami; prints, pacing, tree structures.

- 2009 (Class A) — Couple photographed a Bigfoot at remote cabin.

- 2014 — Rabbit Lake screams.

- 1970 — Yellow Top sighting at Cobalt Lode Mine by 27 workers.

- Early 1900s–1970s — Multiple Yellow Top incidents — miners, settlers, school bus driver.

- 2011 — Growls and screams at Lake Temagami.

SUDBURY & DISTRICT

- 2013 (Winter) — Trout Lake trackway — one of Ontario's best documented.

- 2009 (Class B) — Winter trackway filmed south of Sudbury.

- 2015 (Capreol) — Creature seen near watering hole.

- 2015 (Killarney) — Screams and running figure.

- 2012 (Burwash) — Large rocks thrown at hikers.

- 2012 — Eye-contact encounter with Sasquatch in swamp north of Hanmer.

- 2008–Present — Long-term activity near Mowat; cabin pounding, pacing, screams.

- 2014 (Cartier) — Vocalizations.

- 2012 (Paradise Lake) — Tracks in swamp.

- 2012 (West of Estaire) — Close-range face-to-face encounter.

NORTH BAY & NIPISSING DISTRICT

- 2015 — Horses spooked during trail ride; large dark figure observed.

- 2015 (Corbeil) — Vocals & prints.
- 2014 (Deschesnay Falls) — Face peeking through trees.
- 2014 (McConnell Lake Rd.) — Red eye shine incident.
- 2010 — Road crossing during moose hunting season.
- 2013 — High-pitched vocalizations near North Bay.

COCHRANE DISTRICT & NORTH

- 1992 (Class A) — Policeman sees Sasquatch at night on Trans-Canada Hwy.
- 2015 — Headlights roadside encounter in South Porcupine.
- 1961 — Sasquatch parts raspberry canes, peeks through bushes.
- 2013 — Four male Sasquatches walking in single file near Moosonee.
- 2012 (NE of Iroquois Falls) — Scream responding to moose call.
- 2012 (Larder Lake) — Tree snaps.

KENORA DISTRICT & THE FAR NORTHWEST

- 2022–Present (Class A) — Multiple sightings & tracks near Fort Hope; daylight crossing.

- 2009 (Class B) — Sioux Narrows bear carcass incident; repeated cabin-area sightings.

- 2006 (Class A) — Daylight sighting near tourist cabins.

- 1998 — Fisherman sees figure on shore near Sioux Lookout.

- 2008 (Grassy Narrows) — 8-foot figure; six-toed track cast.

- 2006 (Snelgrove Lake) — Rock throwing, screams; featured on MonsterQuest.

- 1996 (Lac Seul) — Large footprint found by firefighters.

- 1993–94 — Rainy Lake juvenile hunter's encounter.

- Longlac (Tracks & feces) — Feces recovered, tracks photographed.

THUNDER BAY REGION

- 2005 (Class B) — Rocks thrown at boaters north of Thunder Bay.

- 1958 — Snowfield tracks.

- 2014 — Whitesand River vocalizations.

- Tree snaps & scat — West of Thunder Bay (2012).

- 2019 (Dryden) — Vocal recordings by family.

SAULT STE. MARIE & ALGOMA DISTRICT

- 2004 — Night whistles.
- 2004 — Rock throwing at Lake Superior Provincial Park.
- 2014 — Blue eye shine, snaps answering outside home.
- 2011 — Old Woman Bay tracks.
- 2008 (Elliot Lake) — Sighting.

DURHAM & SOUTHERN FRINGE

- 2013 — Off-roaders hear knocking & growling.
- 2014 — Prints in Lanark field.

EASTERN ONTARIO

- 2003 (Class A) — Toronto police officer's close encounter while moose hunting.
- 2004 (Class A) — Road crossing by trucker.

- 2006 (Class A) — Father & son roadside sighting.

CENTRAL COUNTIES

- 1995–2015 — Multiple incidents: heavy footsteps around tent, rock throwing, Awenda Park sighting, strange vocals.

- 2013 (Tweed) — Large ape-like figure on trail.

- 2014 (Lanark) — Snow tracks.

PARRY SOUND DISTRICT

- 1978 — Two workers see Sasquatch at ORF plant window.

- 2014 — Vocals at Bear Lake.

- Pre-2010 — Naiscoot Lake dark figure on tracks.

- 2024 — Naiscoot Lake Island vocalizations (two hunters).

SOUTHWEST COUNTIES

- 2015 (Grand Bend) — Screams.

- 2015 (Woodstock) — Footprint.

- 2013 — Water Treatment Plant worker sighting (Brant).

SIMCOE COUNTY

- 2013 — Midnight vocalizations in New Tecumseth.

NIAGARA REGION

- 2013 — Prints on Lake Gibson shoreline.

LENNOX & ADDINGTON

- 2013 (Puzzle Lake) — Boulder thrown into water.

PETERBOROUGH COUNTY / KAWARTHAS

- Ongoing activity
- Tracks documented
- Investigators spent a night with witnesses

HASTINGS COUNTY

- 1988 — Child sees Sasquatch press hands against tent.

HALTON COUNTY

- 2013 — 15–16" mud track in Burns Conservation Area.

HUNTSVILLE REGION

- 2010 — Daylight sighting.

TIMMINS REGION

- 2012 — Pre-dawn growl, daylight sighting.
- 2011 — Nighttime road-crossing on Hwy 101.

FINAL NOTE

This appendix will continue to evolve as:

- new reports come in,

- witnesses step forward,
- investigations conclude, and
- long-term research sites reveal patterns.

Ontario is still an open file —
and this database is just the beginning.

APPENDIX B — Indigenous Lore & Historical Accounts

A Cultural and Historical Context for the Ontario Bigfoot Phenomenon

A NOTE BEFORE WE BEGIN

Indigenous stories are not "Bigfoot stories."

They are cultural knowledge, passed from Elders to the next generation, carrying teachings, warnings, and spiritual meaning. They were never meant to be dissected, sensationalized, or used as "proof" to support modern theories.

This appendix approaches the subject with deep respect, acknowledging:

- Indigenous nations have lived with the land for thousands of years.

- Their knowledge predates every European account by millennia.

- Their stories often describe beings that resemble what we now call Bigfoot — but through a cultural lens built from relationship, not investigation.

This is not a catalogue of legends.
It is a contextual bridge connecting modern sightings to the older, wider story of this land.

Ontario is not discovering Bigfoot.
Ontario is catching up to knowledge that has existed far longer than any of us.

1. THE ANISHINAABE GIANTS — THE "WENDIGO," "SABE," AND "WIHTIKO"

Across Ontario, the Anishinaabe nations — Ojibwe, Oji-Cree, Odawa, and Algonquin — speak of two distinct beings often misunderstood by outsiders.

Understanding the difference is essential.

1.1 THE WENDIGO / WIHTIKO — A SPIRIT OF HUNGER (NOT BIGFOOT)

This being appears in:

- Ojibwe
- Cree
- Oji-Cree
- Algonquin

It represents:

- cannibalistic greed
- winter starvation
- loss of humanity
- destructive hunger

It is not a physical creature and has no connection to Bigfoot.

Many outsiders confuse the Wendigo with Sasquatch — this is incorrect and culturally insensitive.

Elders have repeatedly clarified:

"The Wendigo is a spirit.
The Sabe is a creature of the land."

This appendix focuses on the second.

1.2 THE SABE — THE GIANT OF THE FOREST

Sabe (also spelled *Sebi*, *Sabae*, *Sape*, *Sabeq*) is described as:

- tall
- covered in hair
- bipedal
- shy
- living deep in the forest

- avoiding humans
- a watcher, a guardian, a reminder to live truthfully

Sabe is one of the Seven Grandfather Teachings, representing Honesty.

Images of Sabe carved by Anishinaabe artists strongly resemble:

- broad-shouldered giants
- elongated arms
- heavy legs
- deep-set eyes
- towering height

These depictions predate European settlement by at least a thousand years.

When Elders describe modern sightings, they often say:

"These are the ones we were told about.
They are part of this land."

This does not mean Sabe = Bigfoot.
It means the concept of a tall forest being is ancient in Ontario.

2. CREE & OJI-CREE ACCOUNTS OF NORTHERN GIANTS

Northern Ontario — especially the areas around:

- Fort Hope
- Moose Cree Territory
- Winisk
- Kashechewan
- Attawapiskat
- Ogoki
- Mishkeegogamang

— holds some of the longest-standing accounts of "Hairy Men of the Bush."

These beings are said to:

- travel at night
- move silently
- steal fish from nets
- leave huge tracks at river crossings
- whistle from the tree line
- approach camps quietly
- disappear when confronted

Some accounts are astonishingly similar to modern sightings.

One Oji-Cree elder described them as:

"Not animals.
Not spirits.
Something between.
They keep to themselves but they are there."

Generations of trappers and remote community members have told investigators:

- They are tall.

- They walk on two legs.

- They leave human-like prints.

- They avoid roads.

- They follow river corridors.

These align directly with your research into the Ontario Bigfoot migration routes.

3. ALGONQUIN & OTTAWA VALLEY TRADITIONS

Algonquin stories of the "Wild Ones" or "Bush Indians" differ in tone from other regions.

These beings are described as:

- tall men

- living deep in the bush

- avoiding human settlements
- rarely seen
- sometimes warning humans of danger
- throwing rocks or breaking trees when approached

Historical accounts recorded by early French missionaries in the 1600s reference:

"Tall, hairy men seen by the Algonquin hunters who live in the deepest forest and leave great tracks."

These are not mythic descriptions — they are physical encounters, recorded centuries before cameras existed.

4. OJIBWE STORIES OF THE NORTH SHORE

Communities along:

- Lake Superior
- Lake Nipigon
- Thunder Bay
- Marathon
- Terrace Bay

often describe "The Big Men Who Watch From The Hills."

Descriptions include:

- silent movement
- boulder throwing
- tree breaks
- avoidance of camps
- long, mournful calls at night

Some hunters told early researchers:

"They live in the places you do not go.
That is their home, not ours."

This is the same behavioural pattern documented in the modern Thunder Bay chapter.

5. DOKIS, NIPISSING & ANISHINAABE-ALGONQUIN CROSSROADS

The area where:

- French River
- Nipissing
- Dokis First Nation
- Temagami

intersect is rich with stories of the "Mishibizhiw" (water panthers), sky spirits, and the Wild Ones of the forest."

The Wild Ones are described as:

- tall and human-shaped
- dwelling near cliffs and ridges
- crossing rivers at night
- watching campsites
- curious but cautious

These stories match precisely the sightings around:

- French River
- Dokis
- Naiscoot
- Sheshegwaning
- West Nipissing

Your research corroborates this with actual trackways and prints documented around the region.

6. MANITOULIN ISLAND & "THE TALL ONES"

Manitoulin Island has stories passed down through:

- Odawa
- Ojibwe
- Anishinaabe

Some of the stories go back hundreds, possibly thousands of years.

The being is often referred to as:

- "The Tall Ones"
- "The Tall Men"
- "The Forest Giants"

Descriptions include:

- towering height
- deep footsteps
- red or amber eyeshine
- nocturnal behaviour
- exceptional stealth
- avoidance of confrontation

A recurring theme is water-crossing, which aligns with your chapter detailing island-to-mainland travel.

7. SIGNIFICANT HISTORICAL ACCOUNTS BEFORE "BIGFOOT" EXISTED

These are pre-20th-century reports that resemble modern Bigfoot encounters:

1. 1700s — Jesuit Records

Missionaries near the Ottawa River wrote of "great men" seen by Algonquin hunters.

2. 1811 — Early fur traders in Northern Ontario

Reports of "giant tracks" near Lake Superior and Moose Factory.

3. 1820s–1840s — Hudson's Bay Trappers

Multiple references to "bush giants" around James Bay.

4. 1870s — Timiskaming & Temagami Logging Camps

Stories of something large approaching camps at night, breaking trees.

5. 1890s — Manitoulin Island

Settlers report "tall hair-covered being" crossing a clearing at dusk.

These accounts predate:

- Bigfoot

- Sasquatch
- modern media
- internet culture
- hoaxes
- popular lore

In other words — they are culturally independent confirmations of a phenomenon.

8. WHAT INDIGENOUS LORE CONTRIBUTES TO MODERN RESEARCH

Indigenous knowledge adds two critical elements:

1. Continuity

Sightings today match descriptions told for centuries.

2. Geography

Indigenous stories map perfectly onto:

- migratory corridors
- deep forest sanctuaries
- river systems

- old-growth islands
- cliff lines
- places modern sightings continue to cluster

This is not coincidence.

It is consistency across time, culture, and ecology.

FINAL REFLECTION

Indigenous lore is not "Bigfoot evidence."
It is land-based knowledge passed through generations.

But when you compare:

- Indigenous accounts
- historical records
- modern sightings
- trackways
- vocalizations
- regional patterns
- migratory routes

They all point in the same direction:

Ontario has had a large, intelligent, elusive forest-dwelling being long before settlers arrived — and it remains here today.

The mystery is not new.
We are simply the newest people to notice.

Acknowledgements

This book would not exist without the people who've walked beside me—on trails, in canoes, around campfires, and through the long, quiet miles of Ontario's wilderness.

To the countless **witnesses** who trusted me with their stories: thank you. Many of you spoke hesitantly, quietly, or only after years of holding your experiences in silence. Your courage and honesty gave this book its backbone.

To the members of **Ontario Bigfoot** and the extended **field research community**—past and present—who have shared the cold nights, the long drives, the false alarms, the real moments, and the unexplainable ones. Your dedication has helped shape more than a book; it has shaped a lifetime of exploration.

To the many **First Nations communities** across Ontario who have shared knowledge, warnings, and cultural insights with respect and generosity. Your connection to the land predates our presence by thousands of years, and your stories remind us that these mysteries are far older than we are.

To the friends and family who have endured:

- the late-night messages,
- the long disappearances into the bush,
- the endless new gear,
- and the stories….

Your patience and support mean more than I can put into words.

To the northern communities—**Temagami, Sudbury, North Bay, Kenora, Cochrane, Thunder Bay, the Sault**—and every small town where someone has pulled me aside to say, *"Let me tell you what I saw."* Thank you for your honesty, your humour, and your willingness to keep the mystery alive.

And finally, to the wilderness itself.
Ontario's forests, lakes, ridges, and deep shield valleys have taught me more than any book ever could. Every quiet night, every sudden silence, every unexplained sound has shaped this journey.

This book is for anyone who has ever stood on a dark treeline, felt the forest watching back, and wondered what else is out there.

Thank you for walking into the darkness with me.

— Timothy D

www.ingramcontent.com/pod-product-compliance
Lightning Source LLC
Chambersburg PA
CBHW031248230426
43670CB00005B/82